VOICES
EAST LONDON

VOICES
EAST LONDON

Maryam Eisler

Contributors
Gilbert & George
Jonny Woo

Consulting Editor
Andrea Belloli

Project Director
Anne Field

Project Coordinator
Emily Bryson

with creative contributions by
Sara Blonstein
Philip Colbert
F K Ranx Germanus-Kunda
Lyall Hakaraia

Thames & Hudson

I would like to dedicate this book to
Ariana and Alex

First published by TransGlobe Publishing Ltd
in conjunction with Thames & Hudson Ltd

First published in the United Kingdom in 2017 by
Thames & Hudson Ltd
181A High Holborn
London WC1V 7QX
www.thamesandhudson.com

© 2017 TransGlobe Publishing

Text and captions
© 2017 Maryam Eisler
Photography by Maryam Eisler

TransGlobe Publishing Limited
5 Fleet Place
London EC4M 7RD
United Kingdom
www.tgpublishingltd.com
info@tgpublishingltd.com

British Library Cataloguing-in-Publication Data
A catalogue record for this book is available
from the British Library

ISBN: 978-0-500-97085-0

Designed by Struktur Design Limited
Printed and bound in China

(previous page) **Backstage at
Charles Jeffrey LOVERBOY
SS 2017, an East London-
based Scottish menswear
designer**

CONTENTS

GLITZ, GLAMOUR & GRIT

Maryam Eisler

My first encounters with London's East End date back to the early 2000s. I had just moved to London from New York and thought venturing 'out east' every now and again – out of our corporate, sanitised lives in West London – would be an adventure. Like travelling to another city, you might say, with its unexpected mores and norms and purposeful differentiation of lifestyles.

It was not quite the Wild East, but different perspectives from a centralised London viewpoint were somewhat challenging. Certainly raw and in your face in many regards. There are lingering memories of wild nights at Les Trois Garçons in particular, where I vividly recall the dark-wood-panelled, candlelit room resplendent with bijoux *objets*. My personal favourite was the venue's penchant for Victorian taxidermy – a tiger if I recall correctly. If you were lucky, you'd be invited upstairs to the *apartement* to be greeted by colourful personalities like Hassan, one of the three *garçons*; they all seemed to be living a fairy-tale existence surrounded by oh-so-antique furniture and vintage gowns, all of which was for sale if you were inclined to buy.

Fast-forward a decade, to 2012, when work took me back to the East End after a long absence, in the context of chronicling the studios of British artists. This time things were on a more serious level as part of my editorial duties for *Sanctuary: Britain's Artists and their Studios*, an unimaginably creative adventure that led to the publication of a seminal volume that was greeted with enthusiasm. My book-work efforts landed me back in the East End in 2015 for yet another blockbuster, *London Burning: Portraits from a Creative City*. These investigative art-based and creativity-centred forays opened up multiple channels, penetrating social layers, particularly of the area's creative psyche. Renewed exposure enhanced my understanding of the East End's intricate and often quirky social, cultural and architectural layering.

But times were a-changin': there were telling differences between my 2012 and 2015 experiences. And in such a short time! These complexities reaffirmed my initial instinct about East London's distinctive character: a community (I consciously place great emphasis on this word) unlike any other in London, tight-knit and self-supporting, comprised of unique, hard-working and out-of-the-box thinkers, all inflected by a stellar spirit of initiative and enterprise – a common thread held tight throughout its history. As the iconic artist duo (and gracious contributors to this book) Gilbert & George once said to me, 'When you live in East London, you don't need to go on holiday. Here, the world comes to us!'

From the Huguenots in the seventeenth century, to Irish silk weavers in the late 1700s, to East European Jews at the turn of the twentieth century, through to recent immigrants from South-east Asia, East London has, over time, been shaped by a multicultural reality closely linked to its unique spirit of creativity. Over the last thirty years in particular, the area has been transformed from a crumbling no-go area on the fringe of the nation's capital into an active melting pot buzzing with creative energy. I would even argue that East London's vibrancy is at the forefront of Greater London's evolving persona, a lynchpin reinforcing the city's international reputation for imagination, individuality, diversity and innovation.

Voices: East London reveals this thriving kaleidoscope by means of interlinked interviews and images, exploring the area's soul by encapsulating a particular moment in time, place and space, highlighted by economic uncertainty, gentrification, cultural evolution and political mayhem. My fifteen-month journey has taken me from Shoreditch to Bethnal Green, Hackney to Clapton, Hoxton to Haggerston, Stoke Newington to Dalston, Whitechapel to Aldgate, Mile End to Limehouse, Hackney Wick to Bow, and even to Dagenham. All are distinctive and colourful landscapes, quirky and memorable, layered with convoluted history and colourful storytelling. In walking this Yellow Brick Road, I had the pleasure of meeting effervescent personalities encompassing high-spirited pioneers, fertile creators, dynamic cultural trailblazers and style originators, across genders, cultures and generations, many of whom I am proud to now call friends and all of whom I hold in the utmost respect.

As to its physical landscape, East London is far more sensorial than the rest of the city: more scents (both good and bad, living side by side), more sky and therefore more light (lower buildings), more flavour (organic produce, delicious no-nonsense cuisine), more water (canals and

The author reflected in an artwork by Mobster

other waterways), more colour (markets and people), more texture (bricks, cobblestones, rusty arches), more space (architectural wonders, depots old and new, industrial or not), more glitz (at times, for sure) but also, and most definitely, more grit.

It would be fair to say that East London is a chameleon that has always embraced change and instigated hope. Big-development blocks may be going up, inducing fears of community destruction and the creation of a spiritual vacuum, but the inhabitants of East London are masters of reinvention, magicians who have always managed to stay in the mix while using the moment creatively and making it work to their own advantage. Here today and most certainly still here tomorrow!

I hope that this book will help reinforce the idea that East London deserves a place among Europe's pre-eminent creative ghettos, with a future that may well determine the capital's cultural direction. This is not a tome that laments the area's past. Rather it offers an ode to its history, its now and its tomorrow, encompassing the good, the bad, the great and the ugly!

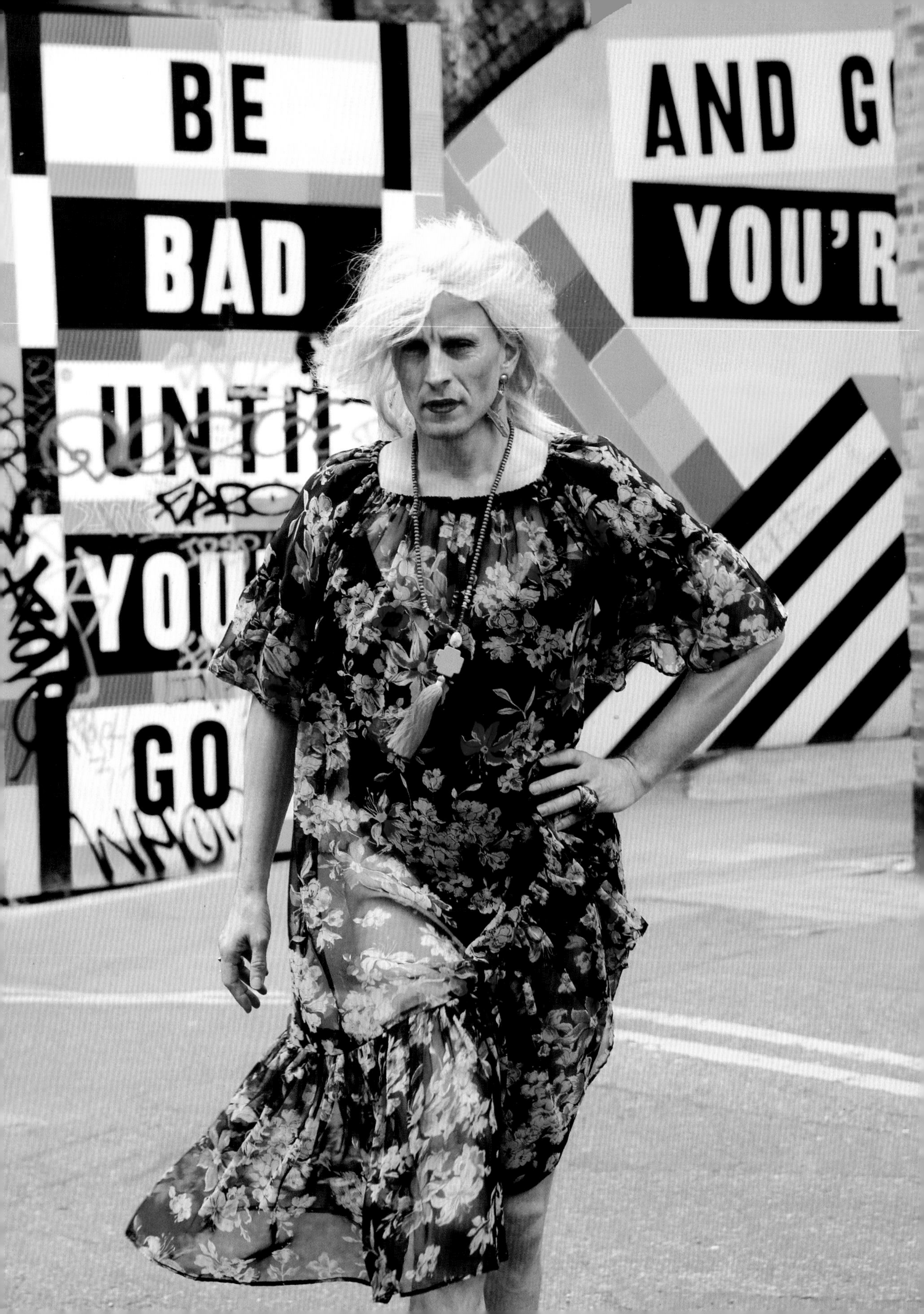
BE
BAD
GO
AND G
YOU'R

EAST END DIARIES

Jonny Woo

'A woman in a green vintage dress posing outside a bagel shop for a photograph being used on the scaffolding of a development of luxury flats on the site of a former children's hospital. Tourists snapping graffiti or "street art". A petrol station is used as a pop-up street-food market, a pie-&-mash shop used as a pop-up gin palace, pop-up shops, pop-up galleries … Sometimes it's as if the whole of East London has just "popped up".

'Men with beards! Men, under twenty-five, with beards. Gay men with beards wearing women's clothes! Children called Macramé and Doily being pushed across an inner-city park through a curated wildflower meadow – in a wheelbarrow. A Victorian law court is transformed into a luxury hotel, and the basement of a Victorian town hall is used for an immersive conceptual lecture. These are the things we use to define an area which we have come to know as "Shoreditch".

'Let's clear our minds of these clichés for a moment and allow ourselves to wonder when and where exactly was the moment when the great engines of the universe were stoked and the world was presented with "Silicon Roundabout", "Stratford International" and the Olympic Games. When the whole world stood up and cried, "Yes! We have heard of you, Hackney". In 1995, in a pub called The Bricklayers Arms in Shoreditch, the world began.'

And so began a performance lecture I gave around the time – the summer of 1995 – when I and other 'twenty-somethings', some fashion graduates, young artists, former ravers and clubbers, Londoners looking for something different to the rest of '90s London, found ourselves largely attracted by chance to what was then a neglected pocket of Inner London, namely Shoreditch. For the performance, I interviewed friends from the time, key figures whom I remembered as having been instrumental in making the party scene, which became a magnet for others, like us. Fee Doran, The High Priestess of Funk, DJ and enduring style icon; Vicky Croydon, born owner of The Bricklayers Arms, the nucleus of the cultural explosion; Pablo and David, who ran the pub and turned it from an unassuming arty boozer into Party Central. Tim, now an NYC music producer, then resident in a warehouse over the road from the pub, throwing parties to make the rent.

Then there was Jim, a Bethnal Green resident of seventy-odd years who shared another history, a local history. An area Dickensian in character, with a rich, varied community, an almost artisanal industry, which to him seemed to have sidestepped the modern world, and a villainous underworld – the likes of which only one who had seen it first-hand could describe.

But … did the world really begin in a pub in Shoreditch in 1995?

I decreed, yes.

There was most certainly a moment, one of improvised living in a big city, in an area which had been pretty much neglected. In that summer of 1995, in The Bricklayers Arms, Shoreditch witnessed an explosion of spontaneity and freedom, which fanned the flames of change. It was a permissive microcosm of hedonism, where people took a haphazard approach to living, dressing and relationships. It was a last hurrah of youth at the turn of the century.

And this became the moniker for this place known as Shoreditch, which drew people to it because they heard about it from like-minded people, at a time when things were still word-of-mouth and not a post on social media. A friend from the time, JJ, described it as 'magical'; they all felt 'proud to have been part of the movement which transformed Shoreditch into the new Soho'. To be honest, now it resembles Leicester Square, but the legacy of that moment carried on for a good two decades. Shoreditch was celebrated, then it became as clichéd and despised as a pre-packed commercial parody of itself: a pop-upped, bare-light-bulbed, stripped-floorboarded, retro, eclectic, bearded, scruffy aesthetic which still prevails today. Then, it felt real and authentic; now, it has a price tag. Real estate is sold off on this legacy, by a woman in a vintage green dress.

A gallerist explained that from the 1970s, artists saw potential in the area that the mainstream did not; this was urban renewal, and it benefited the whole area. Now she sees developers exploiting this potential at an unprecedented, exponential rate. And she says that if we don't hold on to these creative pockets, East London could lose its soul, likening it to what happened in Notting Hill. New people arrive and it's like we've seen them before, but they're different to us, and our landmarks are lost and our memories are hidden and it's easy to feel displaced.

The streets were empty and we were like these mad pirates that turned up … running round the streets and in and out of buildings and climbing up and down scaffolding and it was like our playground. We used to come out on the streets and go shhh and just listen. And it was that quiet round there, so quiet that you could hear a little bit of faint music off somewhere, and we would walk off and find it and go up and knock on the door and go in. Coz it was like that, because if you were from around there you were similar to them …
– Fee Doran (aka The High Priestess of Funk)

LONG LIVE THE EAST END

Gilbert & George

We settled in the East End of London in the mid-1960s.
Being country bumpkins, we were instantly entranced
by the tramps, the prostitutes, the last of the spivs,
the trespassing city gents, the long-lost, the cockneys,
the Jews, the Christians, the Muslims, the heathens,
the Maltese, the beyond-it-all, the down-and-out
ex-servicemen, the posh vicar, the cheeky chappies,
the ex-cons, the odd toff, the navvies, the market porters,
the political nutters, the roughs, the rough bars, the
decadent lorry parks, the fabulous Market Cafe, the
old soaks, the young rent, the light and the beauty of
the nostalgia of the bygone days in this wild and
wonderful magic modern world.

We found that everything of life was around us.
A colourful smelly noisy cosmology of striving struggling
living humanity.

We loved it then, we love it now and we love the way in
which it is changing by the day. It encapsulates all that
we love of the past, present and future Eternal life.
Long live the East End. May God bless the East End.

with love always and all ways

Gilbert & George

In the 65th year of the Reign of
Queen Elizabeth the Second.

Gilbert & George on Fournier Street before the graffiti-laden shopfront of number 33A, S. Schwartz. The Grade II listed houses on either side were built soon after 1725, with a passageway between them to Worrall's Yard, home of the prominent builder Samuel Worrall. The long-gone passageway and the house's façade are concealed behind rebuilt frontage displaying S. Schwartz's sign, a reminder of the influx of Jewish immigrants to the East End in the 1800s

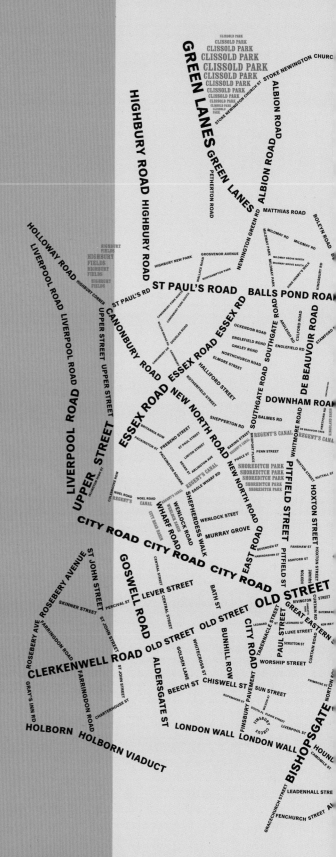

'THE SOUL OF THIS AREA HAS MOVED OUT, BUT WHAT YOU GET IS AN ALTERNATIVE, PROGRESSIVE, OPEN-MINDED, MULTICULTURAL MELTING POT OF YOUTHFUL IDEAS'

CHRISTIAAN NAGEL,
STREET ARTIST

THE BIKE SHED

Anthony 'Dutch' van Someren & Vikki van Someren, Founders

When and why did you start The Bike Shed?
Anthony: The Bike Shed has been around for about five years. It was all about celebrating this new-wave custom motorcycle scene. What we did was celebrate the underdog, the shed-builders, and put them alongside the professional builders to make everyone equal. That developed into pop-up exhibitions, which we did initially in Shoreditch until they got too big and moved to Tobacco Dock. We had ten thousand people at the last event in Tobacco Dock and eighty-five hundred people at the last event in Paris. (This year we will probably have three events in London, Paris and Milan.) When we did our events, nobody wanted them to be over. People asked, 'Is this a permanent space? Can I come every weekend?' That sowed the seed. After going from being an amateur blog to being more of a business, we decided to take the plunge, find the space and create a full-time bike-shed motorcycle club with everything in it: a shop, a gallery, a restaurant, a bar, a barber shop …

Is it members only?
Anthony: We have about 450 members. You don't have to be a member to come in, but membership has some privileges.

We seem to be witnessing a revival of the whole bike scene, alongside its sense of belonging and camaraderie. It's always been big in the US; what about the UK?
Anthony: It's growing. There are fewer motorcycle-drivers in the UK than in most other countries because

Partners in business and life, Vikki and Anthony 'Dutch' van Someren (opposite) **opened The Bike Shed in a 1,200-square-metre space across four renovated arches under Old Street's mainline railway bridge. The Bike Shed has built its reputation through events and the largest independent motorcycle blog in the world. 'We have a lot of evenings with live music, bikes and beer,' explains Dutch; there is space for up to sixty bikes to park at the venue** (left)

the weather is bad and licensing and insurance are incredibly expensive. But the scene is growing because it's not all about bikes. People have a desire to escape from the digital back into the analogue. They also want to do things that define them, and motorcycling, like snowboarding or skiing, is one of those pursuits that people see as slightly dangerous but one that defines you. Everyone belongs to this global village, but that's a bit boring. This allows you to stand up and be more individual.

Why do you think the concept is popular in East London and not elsewhere in London?
Anthony: Something like this needs to be in a place where there's a bit of dirt next door to a bit of clean. This is where City boys on bikes clash and meet with twenty-year-olds on cheap choppers. It's a place where the

leveller, the benchmark, is two wheels. That needs to be classless and without too much pomp. A little bit like this venue, which is bare brick arches filled with quite posh furniture. Shoreditch is the same; it's about nice places next door to filthy places!
Vikki: This area just naturally has a creative, cultural feel to it, which is exactly what we're trying to bring to the table. The original 59 Club was up the road, so Shoreditch has a lot of biking-scene heritage. We love the fact that on a Sunday you'll get bikers but you'll also get old ladies coming from the Columbia Road Flower Market. That's what The Bike Shed is about: celebrating creativity, culture, individuality, motorbikes and just cool stuff. It's about creating a positive association with bikers. When we do our shows, it's important to us that women, children and all people feel safe and happy in this space – and that the food is good.

'Everyone belongs to this global village, but that's a bit boring. This [place] allows [you] to stand up and be more individual'

Vikki (opposite) **perches on a vintage sofa at The Bike Shed Motorcycle Club (BSMC), a full-time space with custom bikes, barista coffee, a shop filled with biker apparel and a barber. Paul Harmer** (right) **leans on his vintage barber chair. Thy Barber recreates the barbershops of old with memorabilia and the traditional finishing technique of using a straight razor to the back of the neck, a splash of cologne and a glass of beer or whisky**

Street artist D*Face's mural on Sclater Street abuts the Rebels Alliance shopfront. A prolific urban creative, D*Face founded the establishment with friends in 2015, offering a coffee shop and limited-edition, hand-crafted items including motorcycles, skateboards and clothing

VILLAGE UNDERGROUND

Auro Foxcroft, Founder

Explain Village Underground to me.
Village Underground is a collection of recycled train carriages and shipping containers that are affordable studio spaces. We have artists, designers, fashion people, illustrators, poets and theatre companies on site. It's a creative community. We have a warehouse space downstairs which we loosely run as a cultural centre with music programming, theatre and street art.

When, how and why did it start?
Ten years ago. I was a furniture designer just out of uni, so the idea was to create some cheap space where I could create. I came up with the idea of recycling train carriages and thought I could fill them with people doing creative things.

Did you get support from the Council?
They gave us a lease so yes, they were very supportive. We're trying to secure a new lease, but because the land values are so high and it's a public asset, the Council has to get the best value. It's quite hard to put the intangibles of sense of place, neighbourhood cohesion, or even just the value of arts and culture, in a numerical format. You're up against estate agents who are saying they can get huge amounts. Hopefully we will get a new lease, and the Council will be able to ascribe some sort of value to what we bring. We have a sister project in Lisbon, but I do want to keep a foothold here.

How would you define the spirit of East London?
London's built of loads of layers so I am in one stratum of many. I still meet tons of people who are striking out on their own, doing interesting things. There is a degree of optimism, but it gets increasingly hard to maintain it with the scale of change. I work on the Mayor of London's Music Taskforce, on music venues that are closing down. It's kind of terrifying. There's only eighty-three music venues left, down from double that a few years back. I'm an optimist, but when you start looking at the data and how exponentially that curve rises, it's a scary thing. It will no doubt reset into a new form.

Auro Foxcroft (above) reviews a report tracing the decline of music venues in the UK. He and his team hoisted four Jubilee Line carriages and two shipping containers (opposite) **by crane to park them atop an old railway viaduct. Their perch includes a green roof (which muffles sound from the music venue below) complete with fire pit. Up to thirty artists, playwrights, producers and start-ups are based at Village Underground's affordable workspaces, with previous tenants including theatre company Punchdrunk and Sink The Pink**

'It's quite hard to put the intangibles of sense of place, neighbourhood cohesion, or even just the value of arts and culture, in a numerical format'

Village Underground concurrently run the Victorian warehouse and former coal store next to the viaduct as a live music venue. A vibrant mural (below) on Holywell Lane promotes the musician NAO. 'We've got a big thing with street art around here,' explains Foxcroft. Their wall, the largest surface dedicated to street art in London, is repainted every three months. Artists experiment with Shoreditch Art Wall (left) on Shoreditch High Street. The Council-owned brick surface has served as a platform for art and even marriage proposals, but its days are numbered as developers are set to take control of it

DREAM BAGS
IMPORT & EXPOR
36 & MANUFACTURERS 071- 3·0 4

Two 1980s wholesalers' shop signs in Shoreditch, Dream Bags and Jaguar Shoes, find renewed purpose as home to JaguarShoes Collective, a group of East London creative organisations founded in 2001 that produces exhibitions, events and products through a café, pub, exhibition space, live music venue, publisher and fashion store

EDDIE PRENDERGAST

Founder of Duffer of St George & Co-founder of Present London

Where did you start out?
I was a jack of all trades. Some children sit in their rooms and don't move; I was always adventurous. My mother worked in the East End and I used to cycle everywhere around the docks. From age fourteen, I was going for jobs in market stalls. I started Duffer, and started selling vintage when I was twenty-four. I had vintage Burberry, Church shoes and suits going back thirty to forty years – gentlemen's attire. We kept the better vintage pieces back and started new production based on those models. What we've always tried to do is mix things that seem diametrically opposed.

So why move to the East End?
The great, the good, the bad and the ugly – that's why! Back in 1999, we found this shop with a crappy façade that was frosted over and sanded off. We pulled it down, and lo and behold we found this sign which had been here all the time: *The Golden Horn Cigarette Company*. The Golden Horn on the Bosphorus is the entrance to what was then Constantinople – modern-day Istanbul. So this was a factory for pre-rolled cigarettes. Loose tobacco would come in from Turkey, and ladies would roll the leaves into bundles and sell them.

Does the East End represent a dichotomy?
I've been around East London a long time. In the 1960s, Brick Lane, Club Row, that was the grittiest, nastiest, roughest part of London, and there were slums all the way through to Stratford. I would have never expected the Olympics to come to Stratford with its filthy, derelict warehouses. That it is so bohemian today and that Stratford's now called a city is mind-blowingly funny. The East End-that-was has gone.

Tell me about fashion …
I don't do fashion, I do style. Fashion is frocks for girls.

Then tell me about style.
Britain has always been a nation of cults. From Teddy Boys to mods, to skins, to punks – forty years since punk rock and it still has the power to shock – to soul boys, to acid house, and that's because of the class system, different peer groups, the playground, where males dress to impress, and girls impress other males. It's the peacock syndrome; it's about looking good. But style is not fashion. Fashion by its very nature is fleeting and fickle. Style lasts forever.

After founding his first street-clothing company, The Duffer of St George, in 1984 with Barrie Sharpe, Marco Cairns and Clifford Bowen, Eddie Prendergast left in 2008 to launch Present. While renovating his current showroom, he discovered the façade signage that reads 'The Golden Horn Cigarette Company' – thus tracking the premises' history back to the 1800s, when the company imported the best Turkish tobacco. In his early Present days, Prendergast would head to 'nice areas' like Brighton and Eastbourne and bring items back to Shoreditch High Street, thus creating one of East London's first 'curated' vintage shops. 'They didn't have [vintage] pickers like they do now,' he explains. Retaining the British-American style of his Duffer days, Prendergast mixes modern young designers with classic tailoring and salvaged denim at Present

'I don't do fashion, I do style … For me it's about the art of dressing without dressing'

JUDE NWIMO

Stylist

'Everything here is acceptable – all sorts of people with different looks and different styles. There isn't one particular look, just people bringing what they bring to the party'

Jude Nwimo smells the roses with Abbi (above) at That Flower Shop, a botanical design studio (left) sourcing seasonal flowers and foliage from British growers. 'Without optimism, what have you got?' he asks. Nwimo dons a Deputy Head Girl badge at the Ace Hotel (opposite), one of the many Shoreditch establishments he visits to sell the wares he locates and styles. 'I've always loved clothes, style and life,' he explains. 'It's all linked in together, all part of the same thing'

STIK

Stik started painting clandestinely in the 2000s, creating large stick figures without mouths on the sides of building, thus reflecting the marginalised communities of East London and further afield (above). A simple style 'born out of brevity, of necessity', the stick figures also portray the body image of the artist himself from when he modelled at The Prince's Drawing School. 'I have always used my body to make a living in one way or other,' he explains. Stik embraces one of his sculptures in his Rivington Street studio, where he's been since 2015 (opposite); before that, he was in Pitfield Street, where he 'gave away canvases for rent'. 'All my murals are about local issues,' he adds, explaining that much of his work today is made for charity

Are you less street and more mainstream these days?
I just did a fundraiser for the NHS. I suppose you don't get more mainstream than that.

Why do you think charity work is important?
I did a mural for the NHS and a print edition that made £50,000 for the Regional Neurological Rehabilitation Unit at Homerton University Hospital. Art is really useful for rehabilitation, brain damage and Alzheimer's. Art has helped me with my own recovery. I was very ill for a long time, mentally ill. It takes a long time to get over that, and art has offered a way of getting out of that. I also had a lot of support from my friends and from charities, and I lived in a hostel on Mare Street, St Mungo's – which is why I'm giving back.

What is your personal relationship with East London?
I've been here for twenty years. I gave canvases in exchange for rent. My old studio on Pitfield Street had a painting on the front called *Art Thief* which was about me partly coming to terms with selling art and becoming a commercial artist. A sell-out.

Was selling out a problem for you?
It was hard, but I came to terms with it. I had to make a living. I was working as a bicycle mechanic and I was a life model at The Prince's Drawing School round the corner from here. I'm not trained as an artist; I never went to art school. I was homeless for a long time, and then I had to support myself. I also worked at Central Saint Martins and at the Royal Academy, so that was my art education – standing naked in the middle of a room full of artists talking about my body, my arms, my hips, the angle at which I was standing, I learnt about the power of classical poses; I also learned how to hold a pose for seven hours!

I guess you had a lot of time to think …
There's a lot of time to think but also a lot of time to feel the agony of bad composition. I was already painting on the street at the time, but that gave me a real grounding in classical composition. A lot of painters these days use photographs and don't get the grounding from working with a live subject and all the difficulties that come with it.

But your art is far from classical. In fact, it's quite minimalist. Where did that come from?
It was about finding a quick way to paint a figure without getting caught. It was a style born of brevity, of necessity. I was painting illegally in the streets from about 2000.

And is that style particular to this part of London?
Perhaps. I squatted in the London Fields Lido for a few years, which was bleak but gave me a unique outlook. I was living very much outdoors. You'd often hear gunshots and screeching tyres in the morning. We were very vulnerable. Then I moved to Hackney Wick, where I squatted in the Intermission. I lived hand to mouth for a while, and believe me, it really matters if we don't make it as artists. There really is no fallback, no plan B.

So would it be fair to say that you've done the rounds?
I've done the rounds. I worked as a road sweeper in North London; I've worked in pretty much every bike shop in Hackney. I even did a little light sex work. I wasn't a full-on prostitute, but I have many friends who are. I don't think I could handle that, but I have always used my body to make my living. I actually think that the art world is not that different. They've called me a media whore, but the art world itself can be whorish!

I love your honesty. There's no filter.
I have boundaries. I value my privacy, which is why I wear sunshades and my baseball cap whenever I'm outside. Anonymity is more of a formality now. It's no secret who I am, but I ask journalists to respect my anonymity. I hide my eyes, as my eyes are keys to my soul. The eyes are also the only facial feature that I paint on my work, and in the end, I would argue that my art is what matters – not who I am.

In 2015 Stik released a publication featuring a decade's worth of work across three continents at Artwords Bookshop on Rivington Street, which specialises in books and magazines on contemporary visual arts and culture (above). **These days he sees himself as more mainstream. His mural on Fournier Street depicts a woman wearing a hijab and holding hands with a stick figure, embodying his belief that multicultural societies can work well (all the more poignant considering the artwork's location near Brick Lane's Jamme Masjid)** (right). **Earlier works can often be found on derelict buildings about to be knocked down for redevelopment. In many cases, the Council has decided to preserve the murals** (opposite)

'I squatted in London Fields Lido for a few years, which was bleak but gave me a unique outlook'

F K RANX GERMANUS-KUNDA

'However You Wish to Interpret a Pimp'

How would you describe your daily life?
It's become less of a chore and more of a lifestyle. It's about fulfilling my creative needs. I guess in the practical sense, I make my living out of Shoreditch and people's dreams. In the old days, I was younger, stupid, very carefree. And it was more of a transient place so you saw a wider variety of people, way more cosmopolitan than it is now.

Have you had to be a chameleon to adapt?
Well, being an African man in London, I'm instinctively a chameleon. Especially when you're dropped in the middle of Holland Park, you find that in order to get on, you really need to take on new colours. That stayed with me all this time.

Why did you move here from Holland Park?
There came a point where I didn't feel that I was challenged. Holland Park and Notting Hill became more of a straitjacket. I've always been that person that not necessarily rebelled but had always wanted something *other* than what everyone else did. This was like the Western frontier, even though it's in the east. Somebody could go be a kid. A place where authority didn't exist, the Council didn't exist, the rules didn't exist, only other outlaws.

This was what year?
1989.

Moving from Cameroon to London in 1989, F K Ranx Germanus-Kunda was first attracted to Shoreditch for 'its lack of authority … as well as being surrounded by other "outlaws"'. One of the first directors of Shoreditch Studios, a collection of photography studios in the disused Victorian railway arches around Bateman's Row, Germanus-Kunda has been key to establishing creative events in the area. He also has close connections with the graffiti artists who paint the area's walls. When asked whether he commissioned American street artist Shepard Fairey's work under one of the arches (opposite), he replies modestly, 'Let's not say "commission". I gave him a wall'

What about the area today? You've said it's less about defining the area geographically but instead about an ethos. Is it about a special way of thinking?
I always found East London to be less of a geographic place. It's constantly moving. It's that idea of freedom, freedom to express.

And freedom to do?
To do cheaply. I believe that's why people have always been attracted to this part of London. As expensive as it is now, it's still comparatively not too expensive.

Are you concerned about the expense?
Not at all. In the same way as you morph, like a chameleon, there's always new opportunities.

Unfortunately, some people reach a certain point of their growth and they see nothing else apart from that. I don't believe that. Shoreditch has always been a cycle. I'm sure if you asked the Huguenots who were here back in the late 1700s, they would say, 'The Jews are moving in; we've got to leave!' But that was two hundred years ago and they are still going.

So the East End is still happening, recreating itself?
Exactly. That's the way to look at this whole area and what drives it, that dynamism – people's ideas.

And how would you describe yourself?
I have no job. I have no role. What I am is … I am the *original* Hoxton pimp.

'It's that idea of freedom, freedom to express'

Street artist Ben Eine is notable for his exploration of graffiti letterforms, with a distinct typographic style. His letters appear on shop shutters, often spelling entire words across walls. His 'Scary' sign (left) is located under an arch on Rivington Street near Ranx's office (above). Chinese-born muralist DALeast is another prolific street artist, alongside being a painter, sculptor and digital artist. He uses paint to resemble thousands of metal shards that come together to form intricate animal-like shapes, in this case (opposite) perhaps a panther

TERRY

'I love the area, I really, really do.
People are kind round here'

Terry has lived on and off the streets of Shoreditch for more than a decade, greeting passers-by on Redchurch Street (lined with high-end fashion shops and unrecognisable from its former shabby self) with the quip 'Care to donate to the doner kebab fund?' A recovering alcoholic, he celebrates several months being sober, saying, 'All I need now is a proper job.' A bright circus-driven typographical work by Ben Eine, *Like Nothing Else*, adorns a wall of members' club/hotel Shoreditch House on Ebor Street (opposite). Redchurch Street itself was a derelict row of Georgian buildings until Shoreditch House opened, quickly followed by Sir Terence Conran's Boundary hotel and restaurant

NICK JONES

CEO of Soho House & Co

What is East London?
East London used to be the City, the eastern part of London. So it's a question of whether it's East London or the East of London. East London has a bit of grit about it. The East of every city is interesting because the sun doesn't shine on the East. Traditionally, the East was the poor part of the city where industry happened whereas now, the financial district, the City, has become the centre of London.

What took you to a part of the city where the sun doesn't shine?
It's shone on us! There was no cleverness about it. Ten years ago, the guys who run Mother downstairs said we should look at Shoreditch. I went, 'Where's Shoreditch?' It was quite close to Islington, but everything was derelict. Redchurch Street then, you were lucky not to get mugged. As soon as you walked into this space, there were big floors of grey concrete, and you just immediately fell in love with it. You could see the potential of the swimming pool as you clambered on to the roof.

In the same way that White Cube had an effect on Hoxton Square, would you agree that you've had an impact on this area?
I think it was self-feeding. London was always going to expand and will continue to expand. People could no longer afford to live in central areas like Mayfair. There was a magic moment in Shoreditch in the late '80s/early '90s where artists like Rachel Whiteread, Tim Noble and Sue Webster were discovering the area. They still come here often. You can wave to Rachel from here; we put those trees on the terrace in order to give her some privacy. In a way, you follow the artists as they sniff out areas first.

Entrepreneur Nick Jones, known to work on hunches and observations, attributes his success in the founding of Shoreditch House to 'mistake and luck' (left). Having established Soho House in 1995, he expanded the group to include an old tea warehouse on Ebor Street in 2007. 'There was a magic moment when the artists were discovering Shoreditch,' he remembers (opposite)

'In a way, you follow the artists as they sniff out areas first'

Are you concerned for London as a city with its changing politics and Brexit?

I'm not concerned because London will work itself out. Every city has a moment where a lot of money has been invested. In London, you can say that's a good thing or a bad thing. If you ask the purists, they would say, 'We don't want anything to change.' But all the artists go further east now. It's the same as in New York. The artists moved to Brooklyn, Bushwick and (now) Detroit because they can get big warehouse spaces. In ten years' time, they'll be saying, 'Oh, Detroit is too expensive!' and they'll have moved somewhere else.

Looking at Shoreditch House, every floor has a personality of its own. And lots of people are running their businesses from their laptops on your sofas!

Life is a blur now. It's the way creative people always wanted to work. The world has become less polished, less corporate and less structured. People connect through the Internet, and you no longer need an office and a receptionist to set up a company. People can work wherever. There are more Soho House members working this way than there were twenty years ago when it was more suited and booted. I'm waiting for it to go back the other way – a bit more polished and corporate again.

You've mentioned the East End offering a constant tension between glamour and grit. Do you think the formula of glitz and grit spurs creativity?

It's a great combination. In terms of what people wear, if it's all glamorous, it's boring. I think rooms need to have something gritty then glamorous; extremes are great. I don't think you necessarily need it in an area, but when you come here, you do see grit and some glamour. Look at the Meatpacking District in New York. It was somewhat magical in its early days, but New York has cleaned it up.

Would you say that the style of this club is a sort of self-portrait?

If there is any element that acts as a self-portrait, it's something which is comfortable and isn't self-conscious. Every one of our clubs has its own feel; I think the area has to dictate that. You go into a lot of places that only really work with people in them. That's not the case here. If you go into Shoreditch House at 7.00 a.m., it has a lovely feeling, but it also works when it's packed.

How would you like to be remembered? Do you even care?

I never think like that. It's a big team effort, and I certainly couldn't do it all myself. I'd like to feel we've made going out nicer for people.

Jones surveys the view from the rooftop lawn of Shoreditch House (opposite). **The six-storey East London outpost caters to young creatives and boasts, among other things, a restaurant with a 360-degree view of the city** (above). **The club prioritises efficient work and community spaces. The converted warehouse's rooftop pool** (left) **remains heated throughout the year. 'A lot of money has been invested in London,' reflects Jones. 'You can say it's good or bad … When you add up all the arguments, it probably all comes out equal somehow'**

Artist

Tell me about your work as a solo artist, as opposed to your collaborative work with Tim [Noble].
When Tim and I work together, we gel really well. It's always been a natural thing so if we can, we'll continue until we know it's over. At the moment, we're still doing our own work too. We've been in each other's pockets for over twenty years so things are bound to get stale. In order to have different experiences again, we had to separate. Tim and I got offered a residency in Copenhagen and won the equivalent of the Turner Prize out there, which was weird. The residency offers free rein of a well-established lithography print studio in Copenhagen for a week. We turned up with an empty mind because we don't normally work on paper; we're sculptors by training. We decided to blindfold each other and started drawing live, which led on to a whole new series. When we came back to London, we took it one step further and lost control again, using our feet to draw each other's portraits. I wanted to do something spontaneous and have total freedom from thinking when working; after twenty years, I wanted to let myself off the hook. Having music on helps because you get completely lost in it. I'm listening to German minimal '80s music, an all-girl band called Malaria.

Please describe the works currently on your studio wall.
They are totally abstract. I started off doing black-and-white. I went away to America for a bit and let a painter use my studio when I wasn't here. When I came back, my studio was filled with his paintings in colour; I was in shock because my studio is generally monochrome. When he moved out, I started painting in colour.

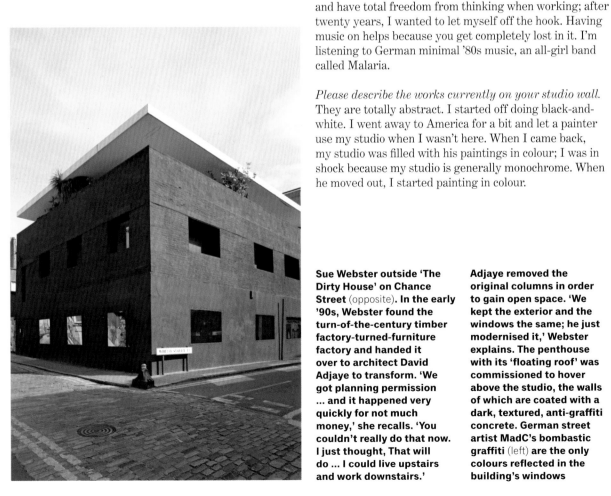

Sue Webster outside 'The Dirty House' on Chance Street (opposite). **In the early '90s, Webster found the turn-of-the-century timber factory-turned-furniture factory and handed it over to architect David Adjaye to transform. 'We got planning permission ... and it happened very quickly for not much money,' she recalls. 'You couldn't really do that now. I just thought, That will do ... I could live upstairs and work downstairs.'**

Adjaye removed the original columns in order to gain open space. 'We kept the exterior and the windows the same; he just modernised it,' Webster explains. The penthouse with its 'floating roof' was commissioned to hover above the studio, the walls of which are coated with a dark, textured, anti-graffiti concrete. German street artist MadC's bombastic graffiti (left) **are the only colours reflected in the building's windows**

'I open the door and it's become trendy. It's full of the people I have spent my entire life trying to avoid'

You were one of the first people to set up shop in the East End. What were your reasons for moving here?
Living in warehouses and using them as studios felt very American. Tim and I were used to warehouse living because Yorkshire's quite industrial. Tim was at the Royal College of Art and we were looking for a studio. We were living in a tiny flat in South London and didn't know much about the city. One summer we went to Hoxton Square and I met a couple of people who said, 'We live in warehouses around here' and I was like 'What?!' That was on the Saturday; on the Monday I started looking for a space. It was that quick.

When was this?
This was in 1995. Hoxton Square was very different. There was no-one around because it was just out of the recession when a lot of print and furniture factories had gone bankrupt. We started in Rivington Street, two doors away from Tramshed. We had three floors, so a studio on one floor, our office in the middle, and we lived above. It was a no-brainer. We were there for seven and a half years and did our first exhibition in our studio. People were frightened to go to the East End. Sadie Coles came to see

the show and was like, 'This is the first time I've been to the East End!' Charles Saatchi used to come and leave the taxi running outside. He bought work, and Stuart Shave opened up a gallery off Redchurch Street, so things started happening for us. I didn't know what to do with the money because I was used to being on the dole. It was almost like the stories you hear of Jean-Michel Basquiat being spoon-fed lollipops and cocaine, but we were fed champagne and chips. Then, all of a sudden I was walking from Rivington to Redchurch Street to meet Stuart [Shave] when I saw this building. It was a furniture factory for sale. I said to Stu, 'Can we have all that money, please?' and we bought it.

Now you have this amazing house and studio designed by David Adjaye.
David Adjaye is now hanging out with Barack Obama and Oprah Winfrey. I knew David from the Royal College of Art when Tim was there. We kept the exterior and all the windows, but he modernised them. Then we built the penthouse. We got planning permission and it happened very quickly for not much money. You couldn't really do that anymore.

What about the area today?

I think it's gone the wrong way. Artists moved here to get away from everybody; I certainly did. It was quiet and there was nothing here. There were no bars; there were two pubs and they didn't open at weekends because it was primarily businesses around here. There was no weekend nightlife. We've seen the whole thing change. The benefit is that the value of this property has gone up enormously and it's now the most sought-after area in London. But the building won't stop; it's changing all the time. I might get a bit fed up of it really.

Why?

I open the door and it's become trendy. It's full of the people I have spent my entire life trying to avoid.

Webster and her cat at home with one of her and Tim Noble's neon works, *Fucking Beautiful*, behind them (above). **Several versions have been made since 2000, the shared theme being contradiction. Webster and Noble's relationship began in 1986; as they are currently taking a break, Webster is focusing on large oil pastel works** (opposite). **The intricate, organic, predominantly red, orange and green *Fallen Angel* mural outside her studio is by Australian artist Reka, while Belgian artist ROA's dominant hedgehog is reflected in one of the windows** (above left)

MARK HIX

Chef/Restaurateur & Founder of Hix Restaurant Chain & Tramshed

Mark Hix relaxes at Tramshed in the company of a bevy of stuffed roast chickens (opposite) **served vertically on pikes in nests of chips. That Hix avoids using battery chickens in his restaurants is made clear by Tramshed waiter Matt's** *Featherless*

Chicken (2012) T-shirt by Tim Flach (above). **Launched that same year with sharing tables and platters of high-quality but straightforward cooking, the restaurant is 'quite communal',** Hix emphasises, adding, **'I wanted it to be accessible'**

When did you get into the restaurant business, and why the East End?
I got into it when I left school because I didn't know what to do. In fifth year, we had a choice: the girls could do metalwork if they wanted to and the boys could do cookery. Three of us boys did cookery, or 'Domestic Science' as it was called then, because we thought we'd be in a class full of girls. But all the girls did metalwork! So it was three boys and the teacher. I ended up working in a pub at the weekends cooking and then went to catering college for two years before I ended up in London.
I moved to East London about twenty years ago (I was doing The Ivy and Le Caprice back then), and I've always lived here. I just liked what was going on.

Can you define the vibe of the area at that time?
Well, I didn't move here for the restaurants because there weren't many! I moved here for the interesting buildings. I bought a loft on Great Eastern Street that was just an empty shell, did it up myself. It was Patrick Hughes, the artist, who suggested I move there; I lived there for about ten years.

You were part of the artistic movement that was happening in the East in the early '90s, friends with all the YBAs …
I used to hang out with the artists who lived around here, which is how I got into collecting. Sue [Webster] and Tim [Noble] used to sneak into the garage and draw on my wing mirrors. Lots of small galleries were opening and there would be three or four parties a week, sometimes more.

Now, twenty years on, the area has turned upside down!
Yeah. It's one of the best places to eat now. There was always Turkish and Vietnamese, but not much else, which is one of the reasons I opened The Rivington. I live on City Road, and in the last two years alone, four hotels have popped up and big apartment blocks too.

Tell me about Tramshed and the reuse of an old depot space.
Tramshed is in an iconic building. It was a Victorian tramshed, so this used to be where all the generators were and where the trams used to get recharged. It was used as a depot for years. Someone I knew bought the building and said, 'Do you want to do a restaurant here?'

It's more than a restaurant. There's a mood … You have serious art on the walls and a gallery too …
Yes, it's a meeting place. People share tables so it's quite communal. When I opened The Rivington, I wanted somewhere where artists could come and eat, and gallerists could come after shows. It evolved from there. Then I opened Hix Oyster & Chop House in Smithfield. I wanted Tramshed to be accessible price-wise, to attract a broad age group. So it's affordable. Three people can share a chicken or you can spend on the big cuts of steak. The idea has worked.

Tell me about the cow in the glass box. It stems from your relationship with Damien [Hirst], correct?
We've known each other for quite a long time. I was having site visits with the architects, but the mezzanine didn't look right. I thought we needed a sculpture. I texted Damien, who came in, and then one or two days later he sent an image of how it could look. Then we had to find a suitable cow. I put the guy who does all of Damien's formaldehyde stuff in touch with the guy we get our meat from in Ireland. I just said, 'Peter, meet Ollie,' so Peter thought we were going to do some cookery demonstration. After about four or five email exchanges, he realised what the cow was going to be for. It had to be a good-looking cow, but it also had to be on the way to the knacker's yard, so it wasn't killed for the art project. They'd be sending these pictures of these good-looking cows with white thighs … To this day the farmer still doesn't know where it ended up!

'I moved here for the interesting buildings'

A long-time supporter of
the arts, the restaurateur
commissions murals outside
Tramshed, including a
piece by Jimmy C (above),
an Australian street artist.
Rivington Street is known
for its street art, including
works by Banksy, Thierry
Noir and Stik

Padlocks dedicated to loved ones around the world started filling a chain-link fence opposite Shoreditch High Street Overground station in 2012. A trend that began on the Pont des Arts in Paris in the early 2000s, the simple 'love lock' concept has expanded to include heart-shaped fabric and ribbon wrappings, and even banana skins!

PHILIP START

Retailer & Designer

You began your career in the West End, is that correct?
My first business in 1977 was based in the West End. I didn't know where the East End was and knew nothing about it. All my friends thought I was nuts when I decided to move east. They thought the East End was down by the river and had no concept of Shoreditch or Hoxton. Who would go to a place called 'Murder Mile'? I moved in 1999 and always wanted to live in a big lateral space, so luckily we found a space with a roof garden. It was a shell and we drew lines on the floor with a piece of chalk where we wanted the walls placed. The story goes that my wife said, 'Honey, there is nowhere to shop!' and I said, 'Well, I will open a shop then.' As you do. We found a shop on Rivington Street and did everything ourselves. We bought other people's brands; I started to redesign later. I am first and foremost a retailer, a good one. I am a designer second.

What is your next move?
The next move is an online shop for Mr.Start and then maybe doing Mr.Start for women. Online is really what I am interested in. Shops are very hard because they are seven days a week, you've got staffing issues, and they are capital-intensive.

How would you define East London style?
It's varied. I don't like sloppy dressing. With us, it's more about elegant dressing. We don't try to be a typical Shoreditch shop. If you're trying to take the style that somebody else is implementing, it is no longer authentic.

How influenced are you by the area?
I respond to the area more than anywhere else. I always say we are a business in a grubby backstreet because it was filthy … it still is to an extent. I used to come on a Saturday to sweep the whole street myself because the Council didn't come on a Saturday and there used to be a thousand people here on a Friday night at the two pubs. When you come in the morning and think to yourself, We are selling high-priced clothes in the middle of nowhere, then – trust me – you'll sweep the whole street!

Philip Start at the entrance to his corner shop (opposite). **Start founded his high-end retail venue in 2002, combining the edginess of Shoreditch with the luxury of his previous West London stores. Mr.Start merges exposed brickwork and custom-made neon displays** (left) **– the antithesis of Savile Row. 'We're a contemporary fashion brand with our own image,' explains Start. 'We're known for our style, our look and our tailoring'**

'We don't try to be a typical Shoreditch shop. If you're trying to take the style that somebody else is implementing, it is no longer authentic'

CHRISTIAAN NAGEL

Street Artist

'I'm a bit of a philosopher, a dreamer, so I think quite deeply about art and the subconscious mind, which is where my art meets,' muses Christiaan Nagel. Even 'suits' from the nearby City cannot fail to notice Nagel's mushrooms on East London's rooftops (below). In 2016, he was commissioned by the pop-up 'Last Days of Shoreditch' (a collaboration between Red Gallery and Electric Star Pubs) to create a massive yellow mushroom as an installation piece (opposite). **True to its name, Nagel's mushroom and the pop-up's days are numbered as the plot of land is slated for redevelopment**

How did your 'mushroom adventure' begin?
I painted with car paints in South Africa and was invited to do a show here in Goodge Street. I realised that this was where I wanted to be, so I extended my visa, met all these great people and started making mushrooms. The mix of polyurethane, fibreglass and a PVC pipe wall when I tried to fix my surfboard caused a chemical reaction and it expanded like a mushroom head!

Does the mushroom represent some psychedelic adventure you embarked upon?
I'm not a drug fiend; it was just second nature. If you do something regularly, be it photography, or sculpture, or surfing, you can get playful with it and do things that are intuitive.

You place your psychedelic mushrooms mainly in East London. Why?
By accident, actually. London has a big culture of the arts and it's where the traffic goes. I saw Antony Gormley's lead figures high on top of buildings, and that stuck in my head. So I made these mushrooms and put them on buildings. Then I fell upon the idea of repetition in colour, influenced by Warhol.

So would you agree that your career has been one big accident?
Yes. For me it's always been about adventure. It's been fun to get up spaces, to rooftops and hard-to-reach corners. It's magical up there. I want to bring joy and visual fun to people's lives. My choice in music is quite dark, but my artwork always ends up in Tinker Bell colours. It brings out my inner princess.

But how do you make money?
I sell mushrooms online and some bronze pieces in a gallery.

Why have you stayed in the East End even though it's become gentrified?
You've got to be a bit active to sustain yourself on the bare minimum. It also pushes you to be creative about your life and how you manage it. The soul of this area has moved out, but what you get is an alternative, progressive, open-minded, multicultural melting pot of youthful ideas, just like in Silicon Valley.

JONNY WOO

Alternative Drag Artist & Cultural Historian

You've been a central figure in the alternative movement since the early 2000s. What changes have you observed since then?
The scene that developed from 2003 onwards was the gay scene but also the club scene. It was a whole array of sexualities. There was a performance element, partly drag-led, in a sort of punky aesthetic. That became a cabaret scene which led to festivals.

Has the scene been politicised over the years?
Politics is in everything, obviously, but the general vibe of this particular scene is that you can do things differently to the way the mainstream does. It's been thirteen years since the first parties we did at The George & Dragon. I came back from New York and started throwing all these ideas I'd picked up into the pot: stuff that I'd written and different ideas I'd had.

Tell me about your New York days.
I was there from 2000 to 2003. New York was amazing. I was always dancing in bars. The burlesque scene was just starting in The Slipper Room with Julie Atlas Muz, Dirty Martini … And there was The Cock, a gay club that I loved. They had naked go-go dancers on the bar. They had amazing performance artists like Kiki and Justin Bond, and Jackie Beat, an incredible drag artist. And then there was a back room where everyone was having sex. And I was, 'WOW!' The Dazzle Dancers and Mike Albo's troupe of dancers influenced me a lot. I was doing spoken word with Brandon Olson. These were all elements that I picked up and brought back. When I went there, I didn't particularly have an interest in drag. I was doing a lot of dance and capoeira.

Courtney Love (opposite) – aka the inimitable Jonny Woo – flips his blonde hair, catching the breeze along Regent's Canal in Haggerston. Known for his performances and events, Woo has become a cult figure in the international LGBTQ community and club scene, galvanising the drag troupes of East London. Though Woo (originally

Jonathan Wooster) (left) **was once a hard partier like Love, a near-death experience changed his relationship to drug-taking: 'I did far too much of it,' he winks. Going sober led him into writing and acting in the one-man theatre piece *East London Lecture*, a celebration of East London's creative development from his memories of the early 1990s**

Woo outside The Glory
(above), **an alternative East End pub he has co-run since its launch in 2014. The LGBTQ-focused club hosts drag queens most nights of the week, with Woo's evenings often focusing on dancing, lip-syncing and collaborations ranging from Grace Jones to Blondie or Marc Almond. Always inclusive, Woo isn't shy about hanging out with local builders** (opposite). **'People sometimes feel excluded from Shoreditch,'** he says. **'The reality is that the hipster-y layer on the top is fairly thin ... Just look around and you'll see all kinds of things happening in every little pocket'**

Have you had performance in your blood since you were young?
When I was growing up, I was pretty straightforward. I'm from North Kent, just outside London. It's semi-rural and a nice place to grow up – all mudflats and marshes. I was into musical theatre and when I went to university, I got into design, dancing and clubbing. Clubbing became a big part of my life and is a big part of my story.

In what way?
I got into nightclubs and into drugs. I don't anymore, but back then I did far too much Ecstasy, which I thought was an amazing drug. In the early '90s I was at university in Birmingham, which was a fairly depressed city coming out of the recession. It had a lot of energy, and it introduced me to loads of different people; I remember feeling that I was part of a happening moment. It had an energy. Then I went to New York, which had that energy for the last hoorah before it went tits-up and got money-oriented. That damaged it more than 9/11. There was another moment, in Shoreditch in '95, when I felt like I was part of something too. People were moving into Shoreditch, which was this forgotten black hole, a semi-industrial inner-city area just outside the financial district. It became a place where creative people gathered. It changed how people viewed living in cities, and it influenced music, fashion and the way people dressed. I remember some saying, 'You don't wear a suit in Shoreditch!'

Why has the East End been so influential?
This is still an area that attracts people that like to get things going. It's become kind of clichéd, but young people can still come and experiment. Now people come and think, I've got an idea and I want to do something because I want to make money, whereas before you might have been like, 'I've got an idea and I want to do this because I want to do it.' Back then it all felt like it was by accident. We had no idea what was going on, and it was totally organic – I don't think moments like that happen very often. People can feel excluded from East London and be a bit resentful, but the reality is that the hipster-y layer on the top is fairly thin. You just have to look around and see the density of housing, people and industry.

What are your plans now? You have your fingers in every pie, it seems.
I overload myself, but I definitely want to do more, especially acting. I think sobering up has changed my direction. It would be nice to think that I made a contribution. There are a lot of people in this area in particular, for whatever reason, that want to feel they contribute by investing their time, energy and money into their environment.

'It's become kind of clichéd, but young
people can still come and experiment'

THE GLORY

Queer/Alternative Pub & Performance Mecca

Home to a carousel of performers and partygoers, The Glory in Haggerston has been a staple of the London nightclub scene since 2014. Launched by Zoe Argiros, Colin Rothbart, John Sizzle and Jonny Woo, co-owner, the pub hosts screenings, quizzes, cabaret and live music. 'When we went in, we wanted to make money, but we seem to do stuff for the sake of doing it,' laughs Woo. 'And that is the charm'

'The Glory is nurturing a gender-upending, forward-thinking, debonair-raising counterculture to remember'

Jonny Woo

Ben Eine's mural *Last Days of Shoreditch* overlooks a summer pop-up of the same name on Old Street. In conjunction with Red Gallery and the Electric Star group, a series of street-food vendors, bars, DJ booths and a karaoke room took up residence on a plot of land awaiting redevelopment. The beach-inspired oasis, nicknamed Shoreditch Riviera, has hosted home-grown musical acts such as Blue Note and Norman Jay alongside street artists like Christiaan Nagel, whose psychedelic tangerine mushroom installation towers above the scrum

Founder of Victoria Miro

What drew you to this part of London?
I had a gallery in Cork Street. Cork Street in the '80s was very much the place to be, the centre of the art world. It was a nice little white cube with a lovely window. Lots of the artists started there, but eventually they outgrew the space and we started talking about finding a bigger space. The idea was to move outside the centre with a space that had more possibility for installations, for films, for whatever. We started that conversation in '97 and it took some time to find this space. My Director, Glen Scott Wright, lived in Islington. He said, 'Let's look in the area because I've noticed some spaces with very high ceilings.' So we were walking around and came to Wharf Road. We saw No. 16 next door. It was owned by an American; he had a wonderful collection of vintage cars. He used 16 and 14 to keep his cars. You could also see the potential as soon as you walked into the building, despite it being very rough with rain coming through. I think he was pleased we weren't developers and that we wanted to do something special here. He also engaged with the artists.

Tell me about the spirit of the late '90s.
The YBAs had been very important, but that era was coming to a close. It had certainly been a vibrant time. It was also the time that Tate Modern was going to open; it was all about reusing old buildings. There was something in the air. The opening here was quite incredible, a lot of visitors. We were fortunate to find these buildings at that time. We also had the garden, where you can show outdoor pieces. The garden was an old rubbish dump when we found it. Everything had to be cleaned; the canal had to be dredged too. It was a lot of work.

What about the changes you have witnessed in the last five years?
I was worried about these new buildings, but we now have a little oasis. It's nicely sheltered and no-one can build on the canal or in the garden so we still have our sanctuary.

Victoria Miro (opposite) **in her Shoreditch space, where Japanese artist Yayoi Kusama's exhibition takes up residence in the two large galleries and garden. Kusama's hallucinations since childhood have resulted in a preoccupation with repetition (often in the form of dots) and with themes of the infinite and the sublime. The artist's immersive installations at Victoria Miro include *All the Eternal Love I Have for the Pumpkins* (2016)** (left) **as well as *Narcissus Garden* (1966)** (top left) **in the gallery's adjacent canal**

On a practical level, when I first moved here, walking around in the dark was quite uncomfortable, but now it's fine. It's becoming more expensive and more desirable. It's near a form of Silicon Valley, Old Street, so it's sad that people who work here can no longer live here.

Do you still feel the old sense of community?
Yes. We still have local artists: Chantal [Joffe] is just down the road and Grayson [Perry] is only ten minutes away. They are quite established artists so they can afford to be in the area, which maybe a lot of artists can't.

Who was the architect for this building?
Claudio Silvestrin did this space. I share the space with Parasol Unit, who have the first and third floors. No. 16 was by Trevor Horne and was very sympathetic to the old building next door from the 1680s.

And now you have another space in Mayfair. Why is that?
It's more for people out of London who are just passing through or are here on business. It's not so much the distance to the East; it's the traffic, which can be quite bad. If people want to see something, we can bring it to Mayfair and they can pop in and be finished in fifteen minutes. That's why we have a little foothold in the centre.

Miro takes the stairs (left) **at her gallery. She moved to Wharf Road in 2000, the year Tate Modern opened its doors on the south bank of the Thames. 'There was something in the air,' she remembers. The Victorian furniture factory was transformed into a 1,500-square-metre gallery by Italian minimalist architect Claudio Silvestrin, who designed a waved façade above the industrial space to soften the bulk of the building** (above), **which overlooks Wenlock Basin**

'[The late 1990s were] all about reusing old buildings. There was something in the air'

TREVOR JACKSON

Music Producer, Art Director, Graphic Designer, Moving-image Maker, Performer & DJ

Have you been an East Londoner all your life?
My grandparents, who came over from Russia and Poland, lived off Commercial Road in a Jewish ghetto. I heard about the streets they used to live in, but they were bombed so now there's just Council flats. I grew up in North London but moved to the East End in 1989 when I set up my own business. I thought of buying a property in the early '90s, and it made sense to live in the East End because I could afford it and there was a community of like-minded artists and musicians my age living in the area. I've lived on the same street for twenty years.

Talk to me about the relationship of the music industry with the East End.
People moved east when the warehouse scene started in the early '90s. Alternative club culture happened in derelict spaces in the area, with Norman Jay and Jazzie B doing their own parties. It was pre-Internet so things were found through word of mouth. Hoxton Square became a great epicentre for alternative electronic music and an important meeting space for labels and musicians.

What were the catalysts for these changes?
Things changed dramatically when the Overground extended to Essex and people came in from outside London. More clubs were set up; things got bigger and more commercialised. Young people couldn't afford to live in East London anymore, or they didn't want to because it was too commercial, so instead they went to Peckham. I used to go to East London as an alternative to the West End; now I go to the West End as an alternative to East London.

What drives you on a personal level?
I've always been inspired by subculture. I've straddled several movements and been involved in various musical and stylistic arcs. I was going to New Romantic clubs, listening to Soft Cell and The Human League and at the same time going to hip-hop clubs listening to Public Enemy.

With the advent of the Internet, can we still have a subculture?
There is a subculture, but the problem is that most subcultures are driven through being reactive. Subcultures are normally driven by the young. The youth of today are quite passive and live in a culture of Kanye, cocaine and Facebook. Everybody wants to be super-successful and earn loads of money. It never used to be like that; it used to be about achieving things and about fighting for what you believed in.

'When I bought a place in the East End, everybody was saying, "Are you mad?"' remembers Trevor Jackson (opposite). 'I'm surrounded by things I love,' he says of his music collection (below).

As a creative with over three decades of experience, Jackson was drawn to the East End scene in the early 1990s: 'I've always been driven and inspired by subculture,' he explains

Is this approach to individualism more characteristic of East London than of the rest of the city?
There certainly are people out there trying to do things, but you won't find them unless you search for them. I'm confident there will be a movement but only in certain areas; everything's become homogenised, and that sense of individuality has gone. So, if you're asking me if there is an East London attitude, to me sitting at my window on the canal, it's full of people from West London. I'd rather someone be individual in Finchley; that's more exciting because it's more challenging than someone being individual in East London.

What keeps you here, then?
I still live here because there is a community of people who have been here for a long time. It's like being in a village.

Talk to me about the role of creativity in your life.
It *is* my life. Creativity has played a role 24/7. I've got a back catalogue of never-released music that sounds more relevant now than it ever did, so I'm trying to find a way to release that. I've just done a remix for Metronomy, and I'm art-directing for Clams Casino, an American hip-hop producer, while also working on international festivals.

How do you see your legacy?
I'm happy to be on the side-lines. In the same way that I walk into a record shop and find something that nobody knows about, I'd like the same to happen with my work.

Jackson enjoys fresh asparagus with walnuts and edible flowers (right) **for lunch at his favourite canal-side spot, the Towpath Café in De Beauvoir** (opposite)**. Open from March to November, the café was launched in two shallow storage areas alongside the Regent's Canal in 2010. Serving a few seasonal dishes each day and furnished with rustic, mismatched chairs and tables, the café has expanded since then. 'We've grown organically in a way that works for us and the community,' explains co-founder Lori De Mori** (above)**. 'A lot of people here are working in a similar spirit, so we're well suited to where we are.' 'There's a real sense of community here,' adds Jackson**

'The youth of today are quite passive and live in a culture of Kanye, cocaine and Facebook. Everybody wants to be super-successful and earn loads of money. It never used to be like that; it used to be about achieving things and about fighting for what you believed in'

STUDIO INTEGRATE

Mehran Gharleghi, Co-founder

When did you start studio INTEGRATE?
I co-founded studio INTEGRATE five years ago. It's a small network of people operating out of London but also out of Iran, where we have a strong presence, mainly in the cultural and architectural domains.

Why have you been inspired by buildings and bridges built over three hundred years ago in Iran?
Because they deal with evolution over time. I am interested in the way that architecture changes the behaviour of its surroundings. I started looking into these buildings because none of them compromised the quality of the spaces or the quality of life for the environment which they occupy. They have managed to synthesise all of these into one integrated beautiful design.

What is your design mantra?
I look at design as a way of life. I've never said no to an idea when I think that my design knowhow can make a difference. I can change scale from an espresso cup all the way up to large infrastructures. What they share is the design method and the values that they can bring. In order to tie all of these together, a coherent design method is needed. That's essentially what I am spending my time doing. I separate different parts of the design and study them in detail, individually. That's how we can change a lot in different scales and functionality.

In his converted-pub studio, Mehran Gharleghi sits on his latest work, a **3D-printed chair** (opposite). The production process resulting in ***DNAted*** (left) 'encompassed public and scientific participation alongside sculptural, design and architectural skills'; Gharleghi sees the 'art platform as one which enables you to fluidly experiment with ideas'. In both his projects and his academic research, he is constantly pushing boundaries to explore where design fits into contemporary society, commenting, 'I take design rules but change the regulations to make things differently ... If you're evolving geometry, you're evolving culture'

You've managed to create a platform where you combine architecture with art and performance. What inspired you to do this?

If I'm experimenting with a new idea, I try it first through an art platform, because this platform allows me to experiment with ideas in a more fluid manner and with less risk. I like to explore visions for future utopias. East London is a kind of utopia. Let me give you an example: our latest art project, *DNAted*. I established a design method that creates an art object driven by a genetic code; everybody came and wrote a genetic code that they chose themselves, and with that code something was created. Out of 128 different possibilities, the computer went through the algorithm and chose a unique one. It explains how DNA principles – the underlying method of creating natural systems – work. People over time took these amino-acid particle structures and glued them together according to the computer's direction. So the process combined craftsmanship, public engagement, art and science. That was the first time I engaged with the public in this regard in order to create a sculpture which had an immediate application in design, in architecture, in cities, in the built world essentially. Utopia! Then, the research and collaboration became a project exhibited at the Venice Architecture Biennale, named *Iridescent Architecture*. It included public engagement but also a performance by dancers surrounded by the kinetic movement of the sculptures.

You are one of the first design firms to apply 3D printing to a commercial end use, aren't you?

Yes. We have worked on 3D-printed chairs and tables in collaboration with Morgan. They will be the first 3D-printed furniture collection to be British Standards-tested, making them ready for public use.

Does the East End environment feed into your work?

Architecturally it's rich, but due to the bombings [during the war], it offers a very defined language of modernism. Cullum Welch Court is a great example in Old Street. It's amazing architecture but also happens to be economical because of the needs of the time. Balfron Tower has lifts for every three floors, so it's a matter of economy of transportation and form following function. I enjoy these structures and see great worth in their architectural merit.

What was your first experience of East London?

I worked in a small practice, Plasma Studio, based in Broadway Market. I wasn't used to the aesthetics of the area and the building was derelict. It was one of the most dynamic times I've ever had. Plasma Studios and the people of East London gave me the confidence to start my practice and fuelled a spirit of entrepreneurialism in me.

Does East London have the potential to offer a utopian vision?

Absolutely, even more now than ever before, because lots of like-minded people are here together and there's also a lot of resources on offer. When these two elements come together, you get an amalgamation of interesting people, interesting spaces, meaningful events and cutting-edge restaurants. I personally operate in a one-kilometre radius! The café's around the corner, all my friends live in the area, and I go running by the canal. All my conversations and collaborations take place here. Here, we are all from the same world. It's a kind of village. And architecturally it's rich, even though the culture of London in my opinion has not really accepted modernism as well as it should have.

What objectives do you seek to fulfil personally?

I hope to make a little difference, and that little bit of a difference in my world comes from the understanding of materiality, culture and technology. The world of technology is so dynamic; I'm excited to use and apply it to the world of design in order to bring personality and individuality while creating unique variations and experiences for individuals. Both architecture and design are about creating an experience, so it captures your mind and your imagination but has so much story behind it. I like to focus on that story.

Gharleghi admires East London's 'often unnoticed' modernist architecture: the 1950s Cullum Welch Court (above), notable for its 'permeable structure and function'. Of Zaha Hadid's London Aquatics Centre located in the Olympic Park, he says: 'This is one of Zaha's best projects. It has achieved an elegant simplicity while remaining fluid and dynamic. It is an architectural icon and brings people to East London from all over the world. We should feel proud that East London is the home of a Zaha building and should make efforts to preserve it.' Together with his colleague Mobin Nouri, he has studied a 3D model of airwaves traversing the Khaju Bridge in Isfahan, constructed around 1650 (opposite) and one of the many 'excellently built and thought-through structures of its time, offering a perfect fusion between utility, design and aesthetic'

'The people of East London gave me the confidence to start my practice and fuelled a spirit of entrepreneurialism in me'

Mehran Gharleghi

DANIEL LISMORE

Artist, Fashion Designer, Stylist & Campaigner

Tell me about the scene when you first moved to the East End as opposed to now.

When I first moved here thirteen years ago, I remember seeing transsexuals walking with their boobs out; now it's just bankers and businessmen. Maybe I'm being clichéd, but people from Essex now move to Shoreditch to live the dream of being cool. When I first came here, I was blown away by the creativity, the street art ... I loved the mash-up, like the cast of *EastEnders*, the Peggy Mitchells and the Pat Butchers, then the Muslim community and the gay community with all these drag queens and all these fashion people that I idolised.

Was there more of a sense of freedom then?

A massive sense of freedom. We all used to dress up, get the bus to BoomBox or AntiSocial when the new rave scene was starting in the 2000s. A few years later, my brother in Coventry was wearing what we were wearing then, but Topshop had taken it and made it cool. All this music had come out of this scene, MIA and all that, bringing it into the mainstream.

Where did you find your inspiration?

I've always loved the cultural groups of the East End. I used to watch the ladies walk past with hijabs and think, I'm getting a double chin; I need to hide it – and started wearing what they did. The likes of Alexander McQueen were doing this too. I used to wear pink lipstick back then, until I met Isabella Blow and she told me to always wear red lipstick. So now I always wear a shade of red.

Daniel Lismore sips tea at Shoreditch Grind (left). Set up in 2011 after the redevelopment of Old Street's roundabout, the diner is firmly rooted in the area's café culture. 'Silicon Roundabout', the technology district located around Old Street, is the third-largest tech start-up cluster in the world after San Francisco and New York City. Lismore pioneered rave culture in Shoreditch, 'creating a hub for people to express themselves ... to get them out of their comfort zones'. 'I'm not stuck in the past,' he insists. 'I want to get that point across.' Speaking about the now, he adds, 'London is a city that prosecutes creativity but thrives on it too. I will never move' (opposite)

Talk to me about the creative catalyst behind your fashion business.

I have a fashion label and we make couture. It was a really creative community when we first started. We didn't think about making money; we just wanted to make beautiful clothes. We got all these artists around us who put in their contribution to making beautiful art. But none of them live around here anymore – this is my big point. People saw and read about what cool things were happening and they flocked here to see it all, but there really isn't much cool stuff left. It's still happening, it's just gone further out – to Dalston. And when you walk around here at night, you get so much trouble.

But it was natural for you to dress up and feel safe, back in the day?

Yes. We used to walk around dressed up. I was the Pied Piper of Shoreditch in a weird way. I used to just collect people. I remember seeing a man dressed as a giant polar bear who had done a promo all day; he'd decided to go out and I was like, 'Come with me!' I just grabbed his arm and took him to a club. It was amazing.

And people joined you and your movement?

Yeah. We used to look around to find cool people to come to my club night. Paloma Faith used to come and stand at the bar when she wasn't famous.

So the club scene you created had an effect on style and fashion. Were you a style-maker?

I was inspiring people to dress up. I was trying to make people live outside their comfort zones. A lot of people came up to me and said, 'I wish I could do that,' and I'm like, 'You can! Come out with me next Wednesday!' I made use of people who thought Shoreditch was cool, and the rich and famous came to see us. There was this East/West mix with Philip and Tina Green, Naomi Campbell, Kylie Minogue, Kate Moss, Björk. The creative scene was thriving and it got into the media. All the jet set came to Shoreditch to party with us. We went to Beach Blanket Babylon and threw the most outrageous parties where you couldn't come in unless you were dressed up. We put on a show. We hired a snake, and they were all looking at the freaks with the snakes and drinking champagne. We had Johnny Blue Eyes who did a show; Pandemonia came from that scene; Jonny Woo was on the decks; Erol Sabadosh did his first time DJing. I liked to collect people in one space. I thought if they bonded with me, they were going to bond with everyone else I knew and I'd make this whole scene happen. We had the mainstream coming to us to get our ideas.

Do you feel like you created a history?

I don't know what I created! My biggest thing is to connect people even if they've been awful to me. I dealt with a lot of rubbish for years from all these fashion people who are really lovely to me now. You had to prove yourself. I came in on their scene and mixed things up, made friends and pinched a few ideas to make something cool happen.

Although the days of hedonistic Shoreditch are behind him, Lismore still flaunts himself at the roundabout, at 6'4" towering above passers-by (left). **Described by *Vogue* as 'England's most outrageous dresser'** (opposite), **his wardrobe boasts well over three thousand items**

'We had the mainstream coming to us to get our ideas'

The uncompromisingly angular M by Montcalm boutique hotel, designed by RIBA award-winning architects Squire & Partners together with 5plus Architects, was inspired in part by the work of Op artist Bridget Riley, notable for its geometric patterning

SARAH DRINKWATER

Head of Google Campus London & International Education & Programming Director

You've changed careers three times. How did you end up in tech?
My dad is a cyber-security developer; I was the arty black sheep of the family. I wrote plays and was a child actor. I also used to love playing computer games, but you didn't talk about that at school because in the '80s, it wasn't cool. In the '90s, I moved to London and began blogging. I was one of the first kids with an email address and a phone. I was lucky to grow up in a time in between analogue and digital.

What's different about working in a start-up?
I tried several positions in journalism, advertising and publishing, but none suited me. In 2008, I got scouted by a start-up to do content management and had to google what 'start-up' meant. I went to King's Cross to Impact Hub and just fell in love. Working in start-ups is about getting things done and blind faith – a lovely combination. I hadn't found that comfort of ambiguity and failure elsewhere.

When did you start working with Google?
In 2012, I got a call from Google saying they were looking for someone who had a certain understanding of tech and a specialist with online/offline communities. At the same time, I began doing what we call a '20% project', where you spend one day a week doing something that isn't your day job. I started volunteering one day a week, setting up a baby-friendly start-up school. We also wanted a space that worked for all genders and backgrounds, and that doesn't always work. I joined Campus full-time about two years ago.

Sarah Drinkwater admires the replica of a NASA spacesuit (opposite) at the entrance of Google's co-working space, embodying one of the twentieth-century's biggest technical triumphs. Drinkwater hopes to enable the twenty-first-century's equally life-changing innovations. 'What I like about this industry is that it's very much about getting things done and blind faith,' she says of the message behind the *SEIZE THE DAY* neon display. Google's Campus London hosts more than a hundred start-up firms over seven floors. A reception area leading to breakout spaces features reclaimed vegetable crates (left) exhibiting defunct electronics. 'My dad was a developer,' Drinkwater notes, 'so I was one of the first kids with an email address and phone. I was quite lucky to be there when everything was going from analogue to digital so I know a bit of both'

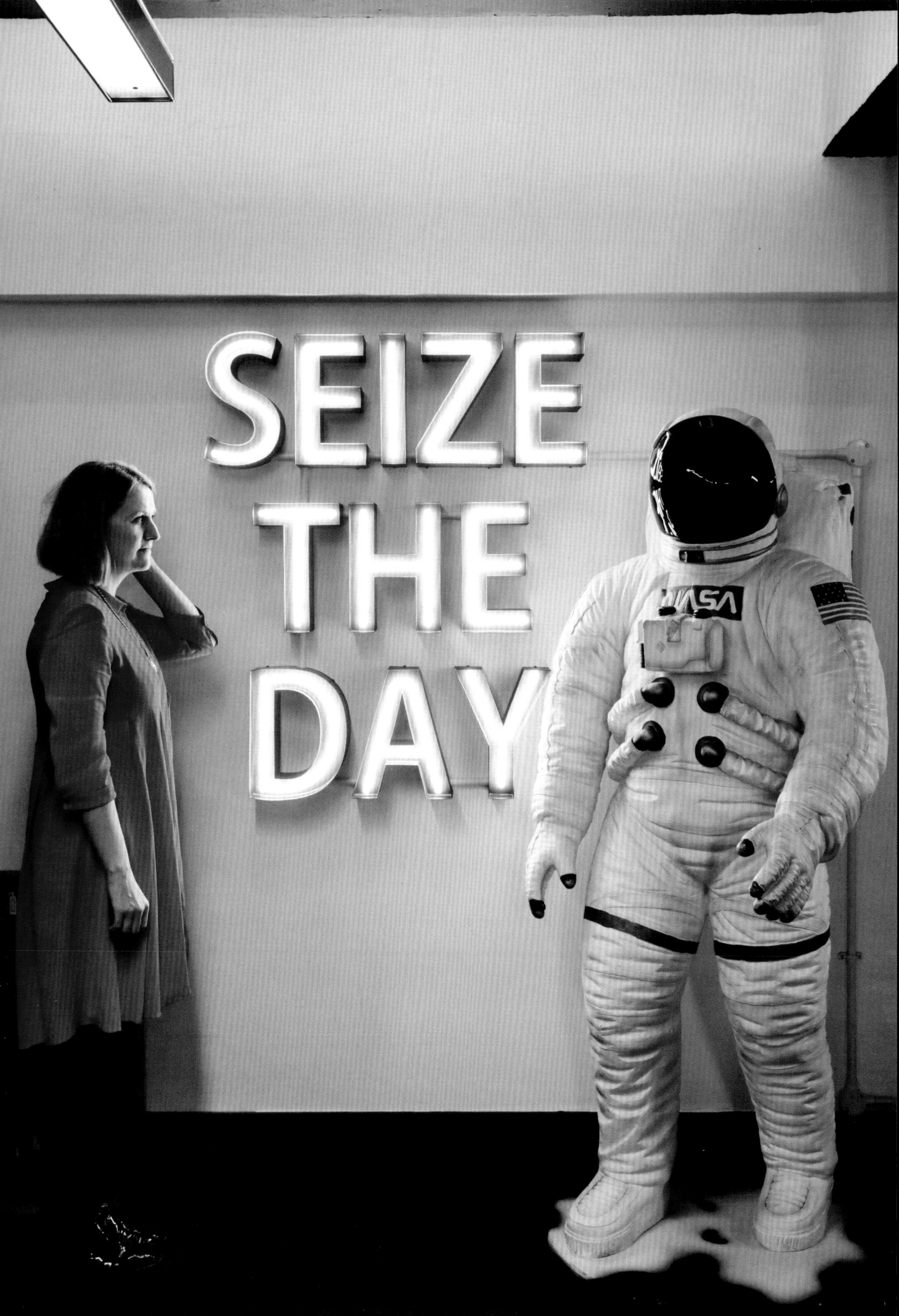
SEIZE
THE
DAY
NASA

How has Campus improved London's tech scene?
Over the last five years, Campus has been fundamental in fusing the fragmented London tech scene. I believe in democratising access, as thinking differently is really powerful. We have Campuses in Seoul, São Paulo, Tel Aviv and, soon, Berlin. London was the first, and people are looking to London, and to this part of the city, as a place where new things come from. As a Londoner I'm proud of that.

Would you agree that London is a planet of its own?
One thing that has struck me is the diversity of industry in London. This makes us strong. But you're right in that we don't look outwards enough. Those of us that work in tech should be looking for solutions, whether that's linking pieces of tech or something to bring humans together. That's what tech's all about: to encourage and share lessons more easily. Companies in spaces like this are constantly working on mission-based visions that marry purpose and profit. That's the kind of thing I get really excited about. CrowdJustice is a group of former lawyers who set up crowdfunding to help fund cases for the public good. Bethnal Green Ventures, which are just down the road, are a great East London success story. They are an accelerator specialising in helping mission-driven companies get further. We're at the tip of the iceberg with tech. The next step is more exciting; it's to do with thinking about the hard problems that we have to face and that cannot be solved tomorrow, like elections and housing.

Does East London's diversity lead to creativity?
I think so. But tension can also breed creativity. I lived in a crazy warehouse where you had to build your own bathroom; I'd never seen anything like it. I'm always fascinated by counterculture ways of living; you go to Berlin and there's a lot of that because it's still cheap, and people are experimenting. I really hope London keeps that. We need a certain portion of artists and thinkers and writers and people who are not doing nine-to-five jobs, who don't work in the conventional sense and who think differently.

What is the future of tech in London?
In the last year, I have been to Seoul, Bangalore, São Paulo, Morocco and Iceland; all have really strong hubs. Silicon Valley is great at what it does, but we shouldn't aspire to be like that necessarily. I hope more companies tackle real-world problems; we must realise that the most exciting parts of tech are not built yet.

Tech entrepreneurs crowd the two hundred shared workspaces on Google's London campus (opposite). 'When we first opened, we were seeing a lot of boys in hoodies,' remembers Drinkwater, 'but if you look around now it's a lot more diverse. That was something very intentional on our side.' Drinkwater phones home from Googlebox (above), a cabinet designed by Jump Studios to mimic London's iconic red telephone boxes. 'I was surprised, but people actually use it for private phone calls on their mobile phones!' she laughs. Google campuses are now dotted across the globe, from Madrid and Warsaw to São Paolo, Tel Aviv and Seoul, 'but people are definitely looking to London and to this part of town as a place where new things come,' reckons Drinkwater. 'As a Londoner, I'm proud of that'

'We need a certain portion of artists and thinkers and writers and people who are not doing nine-to-five jobs, who don't work in the conventional sense and who think differently'

LYALL HAKARAIA

Fashion Designer & Owner of VFD club

How do you relate to your neighbourhood?
I am a nightclub owner. I'm most interested in this community because I've been here for twenty years now. My daughter grew up here. So I'd rather be seen as someone who is part of the community and doing something within the community rather than just as a club owner. I make clothes, I do lots of things. Being alive is important.

Why did you choose to set up shop in the East?
What I liked about this area is that there was a sense of community. There's the Turkish community, the West African community, the Central African community, Europeans – it's such a great mix. The other reason I moved here is that it was easy to be an artist and function as an artist. I lived in a squat. It's one of those things that doesn't happen anymore for young artists, but it was really important. We lived in a beautiful big house, we had our own garden, we made a treehouse, and we grew our own vegetables. We would help the elderly people who couldn't go shopping. We had one neighbour called 'The Walrus'; she was great. She smoked continuously and had a yellow line from her teeth up across her eye up into her hair. She would tell the most fantastic stories, warning people not to come into our house because she would steal their eyeballs or come back for their lashes later. I've lived in North London, West London and South London; the community that I found here was much more accepting, exciting and diverse.

What is the story of East London today?
The story of East London today is that it's rapidly changing. It has gone through that phase where it was poor, then it was poor and interesting, then it was poor and interesting and relevant, and then it became relevant and slightly more expensive. Now it's just becoming a little bit more expensive. Obviously there are people who grew up here, who are bringing up children here, so those small cheap places still do exist, but now you are getting people who are coming here purely because it's part of a tourist route. They don't understand the culture that's been here. That's the potential conflict.

Lyall Hakaraia outside the Ottoman-style Aziziye Mosque in Stoke Newington (opposite)**, which was originally built as a cinema in 1913. Today, it hosts a restaurant, a wedding hall, halal butchers and an education centre alongside the mosque itself. Hakaraia has dedicated the basement of his house to art and fashion. Dubbed VFD (formerly Vogue Fabrics), it is a 'haberdashery hacienda by day, by night a cultural helter-skelter' offering a platform for new talent and the very best in music and mayhem. Hakaraia organises rolling window exhibits showcasing work by 2D and moving-image creatives. One 2016 show, *YOU ARE HERE*, presented a collection of photographic nudes that spoke about empowerment in cities** (below)

What about creativity? Does it still have a say in East London?
Creativity is definitely still here. Again, that's sort of changing. There are no squats. When I was living in a squat, it didn't really matter if I made £300 or £30 because I could eat on £30 and I could still make things on £40. Obviously that's not the case now. So that's a big change. Having to make money is much more important. People used to have parties in their squats or have performances. It didn't really matter if you were engaging with three people or three hundred people. People were able to find their way through it all. I worked, another guy was in a band, another one was an artist and another a writer. In that squat there were lots of different things happening, whether inside or outside the building. That was important.

You get to see different layers of society going through your door, but you also get to see generational layers …
The new generation is trying to make its own rules and trying to find its own way. People aren't looking to the '70s and saying, 'Let's make a new Studio 54' or at the '80s and looking at performance artists like Leigh Bowery. People are definitely aware of these characters, but they're not trying to emulate them. They're trying to find their own way.

Is there or has there been a specific subculture here?
There's a subculture that I would have identified twenty years ago as quite dark, quite underground, quite experimental, fairly free-form.

And how would you define your own mission?
I'm in a very unique place. Dalston is an important cultural centre at the moment and I have a space. We've been running spoken-word nights here for the past couple of years, and they're getting more popular with a huge diversity of people mixing quite happily. Also, we're starting up a new film club, and obviously the south-east and probably London alone is producing tens of thousands of graduates. So we've hit on the idea of doing films in short seasons, talking about social issues, whether about Calais and refugees, and homelessness, or gender and sexuality, or gentrification and housing, or corruption. There's a lot of that, and if you're a film-maker you want to make it about something that is interesting. Politics is the most interesting thing at the moment, not fashion or music. So that's what the kids are responding to, and obviously they want to be relevant. We can be a platform for that, really encourage that. I want to be a focal point for other voices.

Hakaraia's home is a tribute to creatives he has met (above). **The upstairs is an extension of VFD, with many artist friends' works adorning the walls, among them a T-shirt by Idris Khan** (opposite). **Hakaraia notes that although creativity is still paramount in the area, priorities have changed.**

'Having to make money is much more important,' he explains. 'When I was living in a squat, it didn't really matter if I made £300 or £30 … People would have parties in their squats or have performances [and] were able to … work out what worked and what didn't'

'People come [to the East End] for a dystopian future experience'

One of Hakaraia's favourite places is the Middlesex Filter Beds Weir, a nature reserve on the River Lea just above Clapton (right) that was built by the East London Waterworks Company. In 1852 London suffered its worst-ever outbreak of cholera, a disease that thrives in contaminated water. The Middlesex Filter Beds were built soon after in an effort to ensure that such epidemics were never repeated. Nature took over when the beds closed down in 1969, today offering a mix of open water, reed beds and wet woodland habitats for toads, frogs, newts, dragonflies and damselflies, alongside over sixty bird species (above)

'I found the community here to be much more accepting, much more exciting and much more diverse'

STOKE NEWINGTON MARKETS

Suleymaniye Mosque on Kingsland Road is the principal mosque for the British Turkish community in East London. An Ottoman-style mosque with a minaret, its 8,000 square metres of floor space can accommodate up to three thousand people at prayer times. Its canteen has become something of a popular local landmark

FAIZA BUTT

Artist

You emigrated from Lahore to London, I believe.
My grandparents migrated from Kashmir to India, my
parents migrated from India into Pakistan, and I moved
to Britain. My views on the world are shaped by this
memory of movement.

In all of London, you chose the East End. Why?
There are more artists living in Hackney than anywhere in
Europe. So it was natural for me to be based here. When
I landed in Britain in the mid-'90s, I found a home in West
London and soon discovered that it lacked a certain depth;
it felt like a big shop. I love living in environments where
I see diversity co-existing with a degree of acceptance.
It makes me realise that we as humans are capable of
harmony and that we can tolerate each other's differences
as well as celebrate them without conforming. This creates
a lot of material for my work and my thinking.

*The harmony that everyone speaks of in the East End ...
is it propaganda or reality?*
Harmony, migration ... these are buzzwords from
politicians. I would rather talk about 'lived experiences'.
I live in Stoke Newington, which has the biggest Hasidic
Jewish population after Israel. We have Ridley Road
Market with its rich Afro-Caribbean population. There's
Turkish pockets in between. We love to enter into each
other's worlds, eat Jewish dumplings in Stamford Hill,
go to Ridley Road Market to buy fish or go to a Turkish
restaurant. If you choose to, you can celebrate differences
with positivity. Culture is not a fossil; it is living and
constantly developing with input from the outside.

*Would you say that the Muslim communities have
integrated in East London?*
I was a teacher in Newham, which at the time was the
poorest borough in Europe. The school was predominantly
migrant children from Pakistani, Bangladeshi and Indian
backgrounds. I noticed that there are different types of
poverty – poverty of material and poverty of spirit; the
latter I classify as people who have refused to engage
outside the parameters which they have set for themselves.
In fact, they feel threatened by them. Pakistan back home

Faiza Butt (above) **enjoys a
rare moment in the sun in
the courtyard of Sarah May
Studios, home to her practice
for the last five years as well as
to graphic designers, fashion
illustrators and playwrights.
'It enriches me to have those
conversations around me,' she
says of her creative neighbours.
'I never allow myself to relax
in this way and I should!'**

'I'm not a social scientist, but my observation was that [the South-east Asian community] felt that if their values were taken away they would have nothing left'

has moved on; it's evolving and modernising. But the Pakistan some migrants left behind is a fossilised memory which they're trying to hold on to. Identity becomes very confused, and for a lot of Muslim Pakistanis that bridge back is religion. I had students in my class who were born in Britain, and they had never been allowed to go to West London. I took them to the Tate and they were hiding, saying, 'I don't feel I fit in here.' I said, 'Your parents pay taxes; this place is yours as much as anyone else's.' Knowledge remains the domain of the wealthy. I'm not a social scientist, but my observation was that they felt that if their values were taken away they would have nothing left.

Your art makes strong statements. Can art be thought of as 'soft power'?
Art is 'soft power', but everything has a power to be transformed into art. It's not art that changes people's minds in our society, it's advertising. My work is a derivative of advertising, the power and narrative of the recognisable image.

As a Muslim woman, you often question things that traditionally you would not have been 'allowed' to question …
The very fact that I'm 'not allowed' makes me want to do it. For example, when you're talking about sexuality, you're not just talking about the act of sex. Human sexuality is a very broad spectrum; everything falls into it. I hope that when I talk about issues, I talk about them in a universal manner so that they mean something for the wider audience. I don't want to be abrasive on principle.

How do you integrate your background into your work?
I studied at the National College of Arts in Lahore, which was founded by the British to train local craftsmen to make export artefacts. It had a strong foundation in Indian miniature painting while using contemporary vocabulary. When I came to the Slade, the faculty wanted me to put all that aside and be inspired by the here and now. I had to reinvent myself, but it was good because I came up with my pointillist technique, which is somewhere between the pixels of a photographic image and Persian miniatures. I wanted my practice to be rooted in my culture and my history. The history of Western art is not the history of the world; the Eastern arts have held a place in the bottom drawer. The idea is that the ornate or decorative is a threat to serious art, that beauty indicates a lack of depth. But you can lay the most seductive traps and say meaningful things through beauty.

Butt strolls past Clissold House in Clissold Park (opposite). The Grade II listed eighteenth-century mansion was recently renovated after residents voted it 'The Heart of Hackney'. Butt pauses for aubergine pitta bread, fermented eggs, *dakdak* and *zhoug* at The Good Egg (right), a restaurant on Church Street specialising in Jewish-Iraqi cuisine. 'It's a very interesting snapshot of how the area is changing,' she comments. 'People queue for miles to get in on weekends.' Back in her studio, Butt sits amid her lightbox triptych *God's Best* (2015) (bottom), which investigates gender stereotypes by presenting men in loving or aggressive stances. 'We live in this age where watching violent, close-contact sports with men beating each other is acceptable, but two men expressing love is not,' she reflects. A collection of ceramic bowls, titled *The Dinner Series* (2016) (below), is an homage to feminist artist Judy Chicago, youth subcultures and Butt's own children. 'Fated to be an artist, fated to be a parent,' she laughs

The *Dalston Peace Mural* (1985) has become an iconic image due to its position opposite the new East London Line station. Created by Ray Walker, its composition is based on the 1983 Hackney Peace Carnival, with a procession just passing Navarino Mansions on Dalston Lane. Trade-union banners and a giant puppet evoking the Cold War are carried by men wearing skeleton masks. A brass band plays at the front. The mural's message is clear. It shows the unity of Carnival folk against nuclear war – the least cheerful of subjects set off by bright colours and the vibrancy of the onlookers

'I LIVE IN STOKE NEWINGTON, WHICH HAS THE BIGGEST HASIDIC JEWISH POPULATION AFTER ISRAEL. WE HAVE RIDLEY ROAD MARKET WITH ITS RICH AFRO-CARIBBEAN POPULATION. THERE'S TURKISH POCKETS IN BETWEEN. WE LOVE TO ENTER INTO EACH OTHER'S WORLDS, EAT JEWISH DUMPLINGS IN STAMFORD HILL, GO TO RIDLEY ROAD MARKET TO BUY FISH OR GO TO A TURKISH RESTAURANT. IF YOU CHOOSE TO, YOU CAN CELEBRATE DIFFERENCES WITH POSITIVITY. CULTURE IS NOT A FOSSIL; IT IS LIVING AND CONSTANTLY DEVELOPING WITH INPUT FROM THE OUTSIDE'

**FAIZA BUTT,
ARTIST**

THE PALE BLUE DOOR

Installation Dining Experience

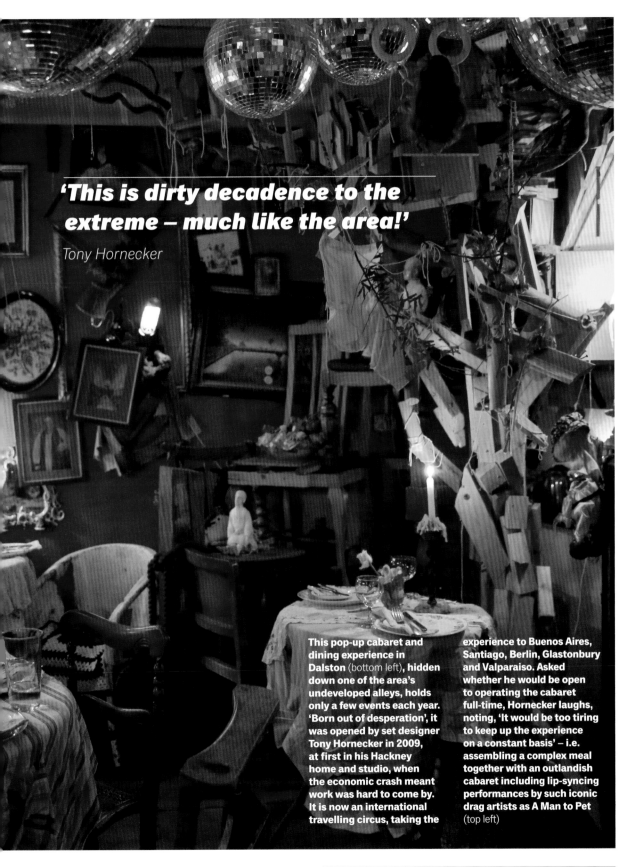

'This is dirty decadence to the extreme – much like the area!'

Tony Hornecker

This pop-up cabaret and dining experience in Dalston (bottom left), hidden down one of the area's undeveloped alleys, holds only a few events each year. 'Born out of desperation', it was opened by set designer Tony Hornecker in 2009, at first in his Hackney home and studio, when the economic crash meant work was hard to come by. It is now an international travelling circus, taking the experience to Buenos Aires, Santiago, Berlin, Glastonbury and Valparaiso. Asked whether he would be open to operating the cabaret full-time, Hornecker laughs, noting, 'It would be too tiring to keep up the experience on a constant basis' – i.e. assembling a complex meal together with an outlandish cabaret including lip-syncing performances by such iconic drag artists as A Man to Pet (top left)

RON HITCHINS

Artist & Retired Flamenco Dancer

How did the dancing start?
Early in my life, I'd done what everybody else had done: went to work, got married and done the usual things like get a house and curtains. But once I looked out the window and saw a fellow polishing his car; he'd work all week and just clean his car on weekends. I decided I wanted to do the opposite. I wanted to work the weekends and have the rest of the week off to enjoy myself. So, I had my stall on Petticoat Lane on the weekends. Across from where I was there was a shop that stored scenery for Sadler's Wells. They gave me tickets to see flamenco there, and after that I took up lessons.

Talk to me about your dancing career's best memories.
Well, I knew Bing Crosby and I met Fred Astaire. I would have liked to have known the Nicholas Brothers. They were fantastic dancers, and of course in them days, you'd only see steps like that in the cinema. I was an all-round dancer. There's no difference between an amateur dancer and a professional; the only difference is the professional gets paid, really. I was a dancer in a Spanish restaurant; it was a compliment for a foreigner to be asked. After you finished, you would go to Peter Finch's house, which was round the corner, and meet Shirley Bassey or people like that. We'd go to all these little dives for a mambo or cha-cha-cha, which is now called salsa. I would jive, mambo, cha-cha-cha, rock 'n' roll, anything. I'd run a disco at The Troubadour in Brompton Road, and people would come because it would stay open till 3.00 in the morning. Sometimes you'd go to a little dive in Fulham Road and the guitarist would be up in the chimney or somewhere because it was so small. I used to always be let in because I was dancing. Paco Peña, who is a well-known flamenco guitarist, attributed a night to me there.

Ron Hitchins on his sofa among memorabilia from his dancing days as well as his own artworks (opposite)**. He was introduced to flamenco when he saw José Greco at Sadler's Wells, and worked his way up from dancing in speakeasies and dive bars across Soho to The Troubadour on Old Brompton Road. For over half a century, Hitchins has organised post-show parties for which he cooked large pots of stew. He has keepsakes from some of the world's most renowned dancers and entertainers, among them Carmen Linares, one of the finest flamenco singers in Spain** (left)

I find it intriguing that you spent the majority of your dance and social life in Chelsea and Fulham Road, but you'd always come home to Hackney ...

Most Spanish dancers learn Spanish and go to Spain, but I'm happy in Hackney. Yeah, I'm likely to die in Hackney. I can't see me moving out. Sometimes I would bring the party back here. There's a story in every party, you could say. If it was flamenco, they would come here; if it was jazz ... All the top dancers or companies came here. I mean, what my neighbours put up with! Could you imagine fifty people in here doing flamenco!? It's different now because all the companies come over for six weeks, but they used to come separately to the Barbican. They'd say something like, 'Oh, can you put a party on for them?' I learned to cook and it's a good job they didn't know what they were eating! It could have been Oxo-cube sandwiches with a banana in between. Actually, that's how I started making meals. When they used to come out of the theatre, they'd only have a kiosk for a Mars bar. I thought, Well, when they come here they're going to have a full meal! Some of the flamenco dancers came here to teach and stayed at my house. Sometimes up to ten gypsies at a time would stay with me.

Aren't they lucky to have had someone like you looking after them ...

I don't ever look at it like that. I always thought that I was lucky. When they'd go home at 4.00 or 5.00 in the morning and say, 'Thank you!' I'd say, 'No. Thank *you*!' Some Cuban musicians come over and when they get to the airport, they say, 'Can we go to Ron's?' before they go anywhere else. That, for me, is a compliment.

'Most Spanish dancers learn Spanish and go to Spain, but I'm happy in Hackney. Yeah, I'm likely to die in Hackney'

Hitchins has always liked a challenge. When he was seventy, he broke the record for dancing Sevillanas, and at eighty-eight he danced with guitarist Paco Peña. 'That's when I decided maybe it was time to give it up,' he says. 'I'm way past my sell-by date now!' On the home front, he hand-carved hundreds of small wooden blocks which he used to adorn his bed (right); his classic car is parked in his drive (below). Reminiscing in his garden (opposite), he says of his boisterous house parties, 'I can't just pick one night. They all blend madly in my head ... Sometimes fifty people danced flamenco all at once! And because no buses ran in this part of town at night, they'd all stay till the early morning hours to catch the first morning buses!'

Site Office →

IT'S NICE THAT

Alex Bec & Will Hudson, Co-founders

Will Hudson and Alex Bec
pose as the stars of the
Don't Hug Me I'm Scared
animated web series,
featured on the Spring/
Summer 2016 covers of
Printed Pages (opposite).
'Will phoned me up and
went, "Hey, eighty thousand
people are looking at It's
Nice That!"' remembers
Bec. 'I didn't even know it

had analytics!' Hudson and
Bec outside Dukes Brew &
Que (below), an eighteenth-
century pub in De Beauvoir
that hosts the taphouse for
Beavertown Brewery. Logan
Romero, son of Led Zeppelin
lead singer Robert Plant,
'began Beavertown Brewery
in the basement just next
door to us,' explains Bec.
'Now it's a huge brewery'

How did your media journey begin?
Alex: We studied graphic design together in Brighton
and were given one week to put something in the public
domain which made people feel better about themselves.
Will suggested a blog called 'It's Nice That', which
showcased the creative world. By the time we got our
first paid creative project, we had over eighty thousand
subscribers. We thought of it as a way of communicating
with each other without knowing we'd built a base of
followers by posting about artists every day. Now we
reach a million people a month on all our platforms,
and we have a team of thirty and a creative agency and
publishing company that work symbiotically. We work
with brands like Google, Nike, Barclays and the BBC.

Why did you launch the publishing side of the business?
Alex: What publishing needs for financial opportunity
is an audience, so we used the agency to fuel and
supplement growth. We believed in allowing access
to a world that was over-intellectualised. We wrote
in colloquialisms about all types of art while being so
unwaveringly positive that it created its own momentum.

*How did starting your operation in Shoreditch affect
your work?*
Alex: We went to Shoreditch because it was where our
audience was and because we were in touch with the
creative world there. Space was cheap and we could share
with other agencies. We moved to Haggerston because we
wanted more space and our rent in Shoreditch, by 2012,
became prohibitive.

How would you describe Haggerston today?
Alex: It's more residential and less densely populated. You
have space, time, clarity and the canal. You have Dalston
not far away, which feels mad if not madder. There's not
much commercial property, but there will be, because
there's so many beautiful wharf buildings. We're almost
on borrowed time. That's the nature of the business now;
you don't have the same approach to longevity. Space
does not directly correlate with the impact we have on the
world. The values, the mission, the tone and the business
are the important points.

*Given that people today work in their own virtual
worlds and communicate online, is direct interaction
still important?*
Alex: We do an event every month at Protein Studios
in Shoreditch. We've had 150 people pay £10 a ticket
every month for four years, and we sold the last one
out in an hour, so there's no shortage of desire for
physical interaction.

What trends are you seeing in local media?

Will: There's been a shift to embracing the tactile while also seeing a boom in the digital experience. There's a lot of small start-up initiatives, which is super-healthy. One of the big things we've noticed is accessibility: if you leave university and can code, you are super-valuable and have access to everything without doing the grunt work. The notion of freelance has changed in the nine years we have done this. When we started, you would naturally look to a recruiter and move from job to job. The recession had a knock-on effect in that people were forced to be freelance more by situation than by choice. As a result, there's a lot more fluidity between people working for decent chunks of time but not necessarily being committed to a studio. We're still dead keen that we try and make full-time members of staff, because company culture is something that you buy into.

Visual artists today are multi-tasking across disciplines; few are 'specialists'. Do you see this organic morphing in other creative fields too?

Alex: Even in our creative agency, we could argue the same. In the past, we would have been an advertising agency, but now we're a creative agency doing everything. As communication has diversified, creatives diversify what they do. We don't feel scared to make a video if we've never made a video before. There is no barrier anymore.

'Space does not directly correlate with the impact we have on the world. The values, the mission, the tone and the business are the important points'

RIDLEY ROAD MARKET

A market in the heart of Dalston since the 1880s that takes place on a pedestrianised street, Ridley Road Market has grown from twenty to more than 150 stalls filled with exotic fruits and vegetables, household goods, bric-a-brac and Afro-Caribbean fabrics

NOEL STEWART

Couture Milliner

In his showroom just off Ridley Road Market, Noel Stewart adjusts one of his designs (opposite). Sectioning off his studio so he can use it as both a showroom and a workshop, he is one of a range of artists, designers and publishers at one of Cell Project's studio complexes. Stewart moved from West London in 2011 – 'This is where I've always wanted to be, whether personally or for business,' he says. The sculptural constructions shown here, influenced by natural forms including floral bouquets, were part of his SS 2016 collection (below). He has built a dedicated following including the likes of Keira Knightley, Lady Gaga and Kylie Minogue

You moved to Ridley Road from West London six years ago? Why?
The Ridley Road Market is a wonderful place to be. I've got my little studio here surrounded by artists, designers, publishers – all kinds of different people. I would love to be in a studio in Mayfair, but it's better for me to be here, surrounded by friends, colleagues, suppliers, and also it's reasonably priced. I live nearby so it's practical too.

How would you describe the sense of community and types of inspiration that you find around here?
It is very much a creative community. There are lots of studios, galleries and high-end shops. The nightlife is also important. All the people I care about and trust and respect are in the area. It is a fun and vibrant place to live. I've lived all over London. I've lived in some very nice places and some not-so-nice places, but this is where I feel most at home.

Is this marriage of glitz and grit conducive to creative thinking?
It certainly is for me. This is very much the heart of London. To me, it defines how London operates. You have £4 million townhouses next to an estate, so vastly different incomes and backgrounds are living side by side. In Paris, for example, the centre was preserved and the margins of the city have become a ghetto. It's much more mixed up in London, and that is part of its strength.

Do you have any concerns about this progression towards homogenisation?
Not conceptually because you can't stop evolution. I would be severely worried if the whole thing would turn into luxury flats overnight. I mean, how many more luxury flats do we actually need? But I don't feel deeply concerned. We will just move somewhere else if we can't afford it any more. That's how it's always been. It's part of growth, I think.

You are in the business of making beautiful hats. How would you define your style?
It has evolved quite dramatically. When I started out, I was looking around for the context that appealed to me most. It was the catwalk and the galleries. That was where the most exciting work was happening, work that challenged my perception of the world. I never thought

'Vastly different incomes and backgrounds
are living side by side'

about making hats – I'd always been making art objects – but I realised through a process of elimination that I had always addressed the body and mainly the head, so it evolved. Because I hadn't been trained in fashion, it was a steep learning curve. I worked in wholesale collections for the majority of my career with the likes of Philip Somerville, the Queen's milliner. Now I've gone to more of a couture structure which works a lot better for me. I always try to create a collection that is pushing the boundaries.

Do you have a grand plan for the future?
I would love to have a shopfront, but it is an expensive endeavour. To be honest, everything is so unstable at the moment. Not just within my business but politically as well. Everyone's been feeling unstable, and the fashion landscape is undergoing a massive transformation. That will be good in the long run, but at the moment it means that I am at a point of flux. Which is exciting in itself.

Generally it's during these moments of flux that something sparks.
Exactly. My autumn/winter collection, which was entirely couture, was a high point because I could actually do what I felt with each piece. I felt incredibly proud. I don't have to always be concerned about my bottom line any more. Instead, I can preoccupy myself with making beautiful and interesting objects.

How would you like your particular style to be remembered?
That it wasn't boring. I am not preoccupied with the social season of the British set. I like the opportunities that it affords commercially and creatively, but it's still limited to hats with feathers! As long as someone enjoys my work and feels comfortable and inspired by it, that is all that matters to me. It's never been about the celebrity factor.

Stewart tests one of his creations on Lucy McCormack, who has worked with him for the last decade (above), helping manage collaborations with fashion designers including Hussein Chalayan, Roksanda Ilincic, Erdem, Roland Mouret and JW Anderson. His Ribboned Cityscape hat was chosen by the Design Museum as 'one of the fifty hats that changed the world' in 2011; he was also nominated by Yasmin Sewell as one of the top one hundred fashion designers. Cell Projects opened a private rooftop for resident creatives overlooking the market below (right) – a great getaway and photoshoot location. Heading down to the fruit stall to grab a snack, Stewart and McCormack share a moment with their tradesmen buddies

SANDRA ESQUILANT

Landlady of The Golden Heart

Some have called you the Queen of the East End. Is that an accurate title?
I'm not! I'm just a real person that loves people. I'm attracted to nice people. Horrible people make my skin cringe.

You've been here for how long?
I was born five minutes from the pub in the Royal London Hospital. I've been landlady at The Golden Heart for about thirty-eight years; next year I'm seventy years old. My husband died. I have a son in Australia and a daughter in New York and ten grandkids who I adore. They keep you young. I still work every single day. I'm up at 6.00 a.m., down the cellar and doing three people's jobs. I've always worked hard, and it's always been like that in the East End. My father was a docker, and my mum was a florist.

Is the neighbourhood as friendly as it ever was?
We're as close as cuddles. We love one another but aren't in one another's pockets. There's a sense of community. It was like that when I grew up. Fantastic people were in the East End. Jews and Catholics, amazing delis and shops, proper good food.

Do you miss the old spirit?
What do you think? You never see meat and bread shops like that now. Brick Lane was fabulous.

What do you think the future holds?
Don't know. Now, it's the world that's gone crazy, not the area.

You have a long history with the artists that moved here in the '90s. Tell me about that.
My neighbours are Gilbert & George. I've known them since the '70s, and in my eyes they have not changed. They're just real, kind, wonderful and talented people. They were the ones that brought artists in here. We used to rock 'n' roll and I never worried about the artists. They had a laugh and I never got stressed out with them. The artists never forgot who they were or what they were. They have always involved me and invited me to their shows, and I'm only an old East End publican! They are wonderful people.

Sandra Esquilant, known to many as the 'Queen of the East End', next to the pub's Edwardian-style piano: 'I love people to come in who can play the piano. It's there for anyone' (right). Having gone through many changes since its opening in 1979, The Golden Heart became a destination for artists in the 1990s, with Esquilant becoming a pillar, figurehead and mother hen to the growing creative community. For the pub's twenty-fifth anniversary, her friend Tracey Emin created a life-size neon heart to hang on the pub's otherwise traditional exterior, featuring the publican's Huguenot surname with the figure '25' at its centre (opposite)

Tell me about the area in the '80s.
This area was derelict for six years during the '80s. Myself and Ely, who bought the Truman Brewery, were the ones who survived. Everyone moved out overnight. The flower, meat and veg market all left, and no-one would walk the streets. It was awful. It was scary. I used to have to work this bar on my own as I couldn't afford staff. The bank took my house and we had hard times here.

Did the artists lead the way in the '90s, then?
This area owes a lot to Ely's family. They had the guts to buy that brewery, and they opened it to artists who started holding events which fuelled fashion and other creatives to come into the area.

Do you have any fond memories of that time?
I have lots of fond memories! I used to love dancing on the tables and hula-hooping. I still do. I had a wonderful dog here called Gizmo who's got a plaque on the wall. He was a human being, and he'd simply lie on the pavement. His birthday was on 5 November so we used to throw him a party with cake and fireworks. Couldn't do that now!

How would you like people to remember you?
I suppose I'd like to be remembered for myself, or for how I am with people. I brought a lot of people together. I love people coming in to play the piano. Lots of people have met in here and got married. How amazing is that? I look after everyone and I care about them. I treat them like my children, really. I can't be nice if people are horrible. I have gypsy in my blood. Sometimes I can be wrong, but I'd say nine out of ten times I'm not.

Across from Spitalfields Market, The Golden Heart straddles the dividing line between the ever-encroaching City and the hustle and bustle of Brick Lane (above)**. A hard-working woman who loves 'dancing on the tables', Esquilant is behind the bar by 11.00 a.m. and stays until late** (opposite)**. Salt-of-the-earth and invariably engaging, she jokes, 'I may pretend a good game, but I'm altogether there'**

'Now, it's the world that's
gone crazy, not the area'

KAREN BINNS

Creative Director, Stylist & Editor

Take me back to the New York art scene in the '80s.
I'm a complete '80s girl. I bought my first *i-D* magazine
and realised I didn't want to be that typical black girl
who listens to soul music, grows up near the projects and
marries a regular black guy. My father was a drug dealer,
but he looked like a businessman. My mother had great
taste, so we looked fabulous; we were about self-education
and appearance – mad bohemian intellectuals. I had that
mystical, ethnic, proud-as-hell, unrealistic way of growing
up. Edie Sedgwick said, 'All you have to do is stand there
and things will come to you.' So I cut my hair and dyed it
blue and put myself in the mix.

*So it was a conscious decision, where you went, who you
hung out with?*
Completely. I went to the Mudd Club and got in for free
the first night, got pulled out of the crowd. That's when
I knew I had something.

*You were a muse to Basquiat and hung out with Warhol.
How did that happen?*
In the '80s we didn't go online; we looked at *Village Voice*
and ventured out to poetry readings and gallery openings.
I was at the Roxy one night, and Jean slapped me on the
arse and I slapped him in the face. I said, 'Your name
is Jean-Michel, you're Haitian, you don't wear socks in
winter, so don't ever put your hands on me!' Next thing
I know I see him in Area, where I used to do parties
once a month. Later he offered to buy me champagne as
he needed a 'favour'. I'm like, 'I don't do weird favours!'
He asked me to look after his ten-year-old sister at his
gallery opening. I took her for ice cream and missed
the whole party! When I came back it was rammed with
photographers and all the work was sold. Jean invited me
to dinner and told me, 'You will never go hungry as long
as I'm alive because I trust you.' I was blown away. We got
back to his studio and that night I met Andy [Warhol].

NOVAN BROS 46
d house for PAPER BAGS
PRICE
TICKETS
of every description
PRINTED BAGS
&
CARRIERS
TO ORDER
CARRI BAGS.

How did you start organising club nights in New York?
I started working the door at Bentley's and the Rock & Roll Hotel. I organised a private warehouse party called 'Soul Boys'. Nobody did it in New York, but they were doing it here in King's Cross. We got together and played reggae, rock, ska and hip-hop. No pop music. All the fashion crowd came. The validation for me was when Leigh Bowery came regularly and brought every English person on the planet. It was such a British aesthetic. I was hard as nails to keep it authentic – no photographers, only the best open-minded people.

When did you move to London?
I moved out of New York once Warhol died, and when Jean died I never wanted to go back. There was nothing creative enough to keep me there. I married a UK citizen in the '80s, we broke up in the '90s, but I stayed and lived in Notting Hill Gate. I was in *The Face* magazine the first year I arrived as one of the top ten black girls of the UK and never looked back. I already knew the fashion industry from attending fashion shows in Paris and working with Andre Walker. When I moved to London, industry people took me in and introduced me.

Tell me about the East End. When did that happen?
In the 2000s. West London became 'marriage-and-baby-carriage' so I moved to Spitalfields. I was one of the first people to live in a loft space there. It was urban and raw, and the youth culture was a lot more active creatively. I started working on magazines, met Tori Amos and have been her Creative Director ever since. I met a lot of music people when I worked for Kinky Gerlinky and *True* magazine. I was the first person they brought in to work on the Spice Girls and came up with the idea of giving them all names and characters. (I never got the credit.)

Tell me about this idea of being ahead of your times.
It doesn't mean it's always the right choice, as you can miss the boat. The industry is filled with 75 per cent non-talented people; only 25 per cent are unrehearsed and original.

You stuck with the East End. Why?
Because it cannot be anything but urban. The houses are smaller and older, and the area is cultured and mixed. It's young. Not that I'm a cougar, but we all need a bit of youth in our lives to keep us moving fast. You must stay in the mix in order to inspire and remain authentic. And you must give back.

Karen Binns strolls past one of the last painted shopfronts in London (previous spread). **A family business based in Leyton, Donovan Bros – *The noted house for PAPER BAGS* – was originally set up by brothers Jeremiah and Dennis O'Donovan, Irish immigrants** who came over during the potato famine in 1845. 'They have kept these places like this since the turn of the century, even before that,' Binns notes. 'The old towns in every place you go will always be the best towns as long as they stay old, at least in the look'

Binns chats with chef Fergus Henderson (right), owner of St. JOHN Bread & Wine, a branch of the original Clerkenwell St. JOHN, which opened in 2003 and specialises in offal as well as the best doughnuts in London. Binns loves the 'urban and raw' aesthetic of the alleys by the Old Truman Brewery (below). As 'one of the first people to live in a loft space' in the area, she remembers 'no shops, no restaurants. It was the boom, the beginning'. Sporting its original name on its chimney, the Grade II listed brewery sprawls across Brick Lane with a labyrinth of tunnels underground, and hosts gigs, shows, festivals and events like London Fashion Week alongside pop-up galleries, studios and restaurants. 'I noticed the youth culture here had a lot more activity creatively,' notes Binns (opposite)

BAKERY

BAKERY OFF SALES

		TAKE OUT	EAT IN
WHITE LOAF	3.50		
BROWN LOAF	3.50		
WHITE SOURDOUGH	4.00		
BROWN SOURDOUGH	4.00	DOUGHNUT	2.50	3.50
60% LIGHT RYE	3.50	ECCLES CAKE	3.00	3.50
100% DARK RYE	4.00	BROWNIE	2.50	3.00
SODA BREAD	4.00	SEED CAKE	5.50	
RAISIN LOAF	4.20	GRANOLA TUB	4.00	
SEEDED RYE	4.20			

'We all need a bit of youth in our lives to keep us moving fast. You must stay in the mix in order to inspire and remain authentic'

Karen Binns

Binns enjoys walking around Old Spitalfields Market, home to stalls stocking fashion, artworks, antiques, crafts and food. The hand-picked array of fashion-forward garments and trinkets means that you can always find distinctive or peculiar items – something that Binns enjoys as a way to 'stay in the mix'

(left) **The history of The Ten Bells, located on the corner of Commercial Street, began in the mid-1700s when it supposedly was the last place Annie Chapman and Mary Jane Kelly were seen before being murdered by Jack the Ripper. Renovated in 2010, its mural entitled *Spitalfields in Modern Times* highlights the silk weavers of the 1800s and East End royalty Gilbert & George**

(opposite) **St Leonard's Church, first recorded in the twelfth century, is a resting place for actors from the nearby Curtain Theatre (1577), and is mentioned in the nursery rhyme 'Oranges and Lemons'. Rebuilt in the 1740s in the Palladian style, its towering steeple was designed by George Dance the Elder**

GILBERT & GEORGE

Artist Duo

What does the East End mean to you?
George: For the first half of our life in the East End, almost every journalist said, 'Now that you are successful artists, why don't you move somewhere nice?' And for the second half of our life here, the same journalists said, 'Now that it is so trendy and edgy here, don't you want to move somewhere more relaxed?' They always wanted us to move and we always stayed.

You once said, 'We never feel the need to go on holiday because the world comes to us right here, between the mosque on one end and the church on the other.'
Gilbert: It's true. More and more, we don't go anywhere else. We have breakfast at 7.00 a.m., we start work roughly at 8.00, and we go up to see some silly television programme at 5.00 p.m. That is it. It doesn't matter what happens in the show. They repeat everything over and over again, so we don't have to concentrate. You just relax. You know what is going on, and you don't have to think what's next.

You have to think a lot in this world we live in, don't you?
George: It is a time to be attentive, it's true.
Gilbert: Ban religion. That is our motto.
George: And decriminalise sex.

When you first started out, you were in the East End and you are still in the East End …
Gilbert: We started our adventure in 1967.
George: It was the only place we could afford. It was so cheap compared with anywhere else, and the landlords didn't mind if you lived or worked there. Anywhere else in London, if you took a room, they wouldn't like you to make art there because of too many smells, or they wouldn't like you to have a studio and start sleeping there.
Gilbert: The front door was open day and night.
George: There was a triangular communal sink on each landing and one lavatory in the backyard.
Gilbert: We didn't have this place yet. It was in a Bangladeshi factory where they made anoraks. It was extraordinary in the '60s with hooligans in Hoxton Street and all these factories and furniture manufacturers, clothing and upholstery-makers.
George: In the evening it was totally dead and you'd get dark streets. You had yellow lights, thousands and thousands of tramps. There were hostels for people who didn't know how to live in the normal way. And a lot of survivors damaged from the Second World War. And a huge group of people who were damaged by the sexual legal system.

Gilbert & George review plans for The Gilbert & George Centre (above), the duo's proposed not-for-profit gallery and foundation in Spitalfields. The Heneage Street space was the home of artist and polymath Polly Hope, who died in 2013. The artists in the courtyard (opposite) of their future space, whose purpose will be 'generally to advance the arts, architecture, heritage and culture for the benefit of the public'

Gilbert: The church next door had a crypt and all the tramps were sleeping there. The vicar used to collect clothes for them and sometimes they used to come out of the crypt dressed like aristocrats.

George: He was so posh, the vicar. The only way he knew to get clothes for these people was to advertise once a year in the *Times*. A lot of people who knew his family name would send their tennis trousers and hunting jackets with yellow gloves. All the tramps used to sit on the pavement and on the doorstep of what is now the mosque. As the vicar walked by, the tramps would say, 'Fucking cunt! You bastard!' 'Good morning! Good morning!' he would reply. He was in another world.

How did you fit into this environment?
Gilbert: We fitted in very slowly. There was a market café where we used to eat every day; we were not accepted at the beginning. Clyde used to make pianos before the war and he did the best food ever.

So what has kept you here?
George: We believe change is progress. People knock at the door and say, 'We don't want any more prostitutes or drugs – sign this!' We never sign. If it is *for* something, then we will sign. As a rule, to be *for* something is much better than to be *against* something.
Gilbert: But the world is going to change in an amazing way. We are all in turmoil.

Are we at the dawn of something new?
George: I am sure of that.
Gilbert: We are doing a new group of works now.
George: A huge group of pictures which only mean something when they're together. Beards, barbed wire, fencing, advertisements and so on. It is our world. The beard became a metaphor. For a long time, it just meant Orthodox Jewish, then it meant Muslim. When I was a child it meant hippy idiot. In the 1850s, the modern world was produced. Men who went out into the world in a pioneering way all had beards.

Gilbert & George stroll down Fournier Street (above), **where they have lived and worked since 1969. One of the best-preserved collections of early Georgian houses in London, Fournier Street was built in the 1720s as a row of merchants' houses, with the upper levels serving as workshops for French Huguenot silk weavers. Gilbert & George in front of the Brick Lane Jamme Masjid** (opposite), **first established as a Huguenot chapel in 1743. The building was converted into a synagogue in the late 1800s and into a mosque in the 1970s. Gilbert & George have incorporated their local haunts into a number of their works, including the 2003** *Fifteen Hang-outs* (following spread)

'We believe change
is progress'

Gilbert & George
Fifteen Hang-outs, 2003
282 x 504 cm

TATTY DEVINE

Harriet Vine & Rosie Wolfenden, Founders

When did you meet, and how did you become Tatty Devine?
Rosie: We met at Chelsea School of Art in 1996 while studying painting. We graduated in 1999 and were living in Brixton, which was a real creative hub at the time. We both wanted to be artists and were together 24/7. When we graduated, we made my room into a studio and used old patterns, fabrics and our hands to make stuff. One night Harriet found fourteen bin bags full of leather samples from a sofa shop and we started making them into wristbands.
Harriet: I was wearing a bit of old belt around my wrist, held together with a hair clip, and everyone commented on it, so we started selling them on market stalls. First in Camden on a Tuesday afternoon and then in Spitalfields on a Sunday and Portobello on Saturdays. We did our first market stall in June 1999, and by Christmas, we'd got into Harvey Nichols, a Mario Testino shoot for *Vogue* and London Fashion Week.

Did being on market stalls help you get noticed?
Rosie: A lot of people, including designers, used to come to Portobello to find interesting things. Pre-Internet, you couldn't just look stuff up, so we thought we were the only two people in the world doing what we were doing, whereas now you know about your entire competition. Two weeks after our first market stall, somebody else started selling leather cuffs, but we had every colour and texture because we had all these sample books for free.
Harriet: We didn't know where to buy leather from, either. We were completely winging it. Urban Outfitters were the first people to order. We only had a limited number of samples, but they loved them.

Did you visit East London as students?
Rosie: We started coming to Brick Lane in the late '90s, as there were a lot of art events and haberdashery shops we'd visit in the Sunday market. But Shoreditch and Hackney Road felt like a ghost town. I used to cycle through Old Street and pick up all the old stuff that the printers had chucked away to make work.

Rosie Wolfenden and Harriet Vine in the Brick Lane shop they have occupied since 2001, a space bursting with colour, energy and creative designs (opposite). **The duo describe themselves as 'sponges for everything'**

'No-one can afford space anymore. That's
a fundamental problem. Space is luxury'

Harriet: We ended up meeting an interesting crowd here – never normal – who bounced around ideas. When we got this space, things intensified. We didn't have any stuff so we just painted it white and sat on the paint cans. We used to have exhibitions every month that were known through word of mouth.

What strikes a chord with me is the idea that your work mixes fashion, art and culture.
Harriet: We're both sponges for everything, and this comes out in Tatty Devine. We act as filters and absorb everything. To only be interested in fashion is something I don't understand, because it's only the crust on what is the nucleus of something much more important: human endeavour and spirit. It's important to be in London, but going outside of London and seeing crazy museums or weird pagan rituals defines the spirit of creativity and ultimately makes your work more interesting. It's about pop culture, a sensation, a mood …

Where does the name Tatty Devine come from?
Rosie: We used to call Harriet 'Miss DeVine' at college so we quite liked 'DeVine' because it sounded fun. We're both dyslexic so we hadn't really figured out that *divine* was spelled with an 'i'! 'Tatty' came from the fact that we both collect things at flea markets. There's this sense that if something is *tatty*, it's been loved as it hasn't been thrown away.

What are your thoughts about the future of British creativity?
Rosie: When we first got this space, it felt like a necessity; it allowed us to grow and bring people together creatively. No-one can afford space anymore. That's a fundamental problem. Space is luxury.
Harriet: London is still looked at by the world as a creative resource, but that's not going to last long if we keep cutting funding. If I had to pay £9,000 a year as a student, it would have given me quite a different perspective on whether studying was a waste of time or not. And it wasn't a waste of time because it got me where I am. Being taught by real artists like Chris Ofili, Martin Creed and Jeremy Deller gave us the confidence to be creative and aspire to more.

Wolfenden and Vine hang out with some bottle gourds (opposite) **in the greenhouses at Spitalfields City Farm, a short walk from their studio. The farm was set up by squatters in the 1960s as a collection of allotments. Close to the city centre while also close to Tower Hamlets – one of London's most deprived areas – the farm operates on a voluntary basis, and keeps a variety of animals and vegetables in self-made buildings. The design duo have a morning meeting at Palm Vaults on Mare Street** (above)**, known for its rainbow-coloured range of lattes from Red Velvet (beetroot) to matcha (green) but also lavender, rose and turmeric (yellow). This Hackney eatery is known as London's most Instagram-able café, with its retro tropical-paradise pastel-pink decor and matching vegetarian and vegan menu**

BRICK LANE MARKET

Running from Brick Lane to Cheshire Street, this chaotic, bustling market in Tower Hamlets operates every Sunday, hosting stalls whose goods range from food to antique knick-knacks. Originating in the seventeenth century as a farmers' market for the area's Jewish community, the market welcomed an influx of Bangladeshi immigrants in the 1900s, resulting in the authentic bagel shops and curry houses that line its lively streets

NATACHA MARRO

Shoe Designer

Why shoes?

For me shoes are everything. My father worked in hotels – the Negresco in Nice – and thought you can figure people out by their shoes. They can have the best suit, they can smell right, but if they don't have the right shoes, you know they're not paying.

For whom do you make shoes?

I like to think everyone, but a lot of celebrities: Lady Gaga, Gwen Stefani and the late David Bowie when he wanted a copy of the red boots from his cover album in black.

And Grayson Perry, right?

Yes. I met him when he would never wear anything but flat Mary Janes and wiggled him slowly, slowly into heels. Now he loves it because I proved to him you can be high and comfortable. I love making crazy shoes, but they need to be wearable. I like when you get a shocked customer who says, 'Wow! It's comfortable! I want to put them on and just go!'

Natacha Marro shows off her designs (worn by the likes of Grayson Perry, Grace Jones and Noel Fielding) on the steps of her Brick Lane studio (opposite). She has been making bespoke shoes since 1992, working with Madame Tussauds and premier fashion houses across the world. It was while studying at Cordwainers on Mare Street that Marro met such creatives as the Tiger Lillies and Mei-Hui Liu and was introduced to her now-loyal fan base. Matching her exuberant personality, shoes are jewelled and painted, with contrasting leather linings (below), and come in every shape, some heel-less, some bubbled, some elongating up the thigh. Although seemingly impossible to walk in, they exemplify Marro's belief in quality and comfort. 'I don't want to fight with the shoes and my feet to be in pain at the end of the day,' she explains

'I love East London. You get that very special, unique and colourful mix'

Natacha Marro

HARRIET VERNEY

Writer/Journalist

How on earth did you end up in the East End seven years ago straight from Gloucestershire?
I came to a Halloween party with this witch on an amazing Council estate in Old Street when I was fourteen. She painted the whole place lime green, and we would sit around and work out if we were a *ground frog* or a *tree snake* or something weird like that. I used to stay there a lot. Then I gave up school and ran away to London with my then-boyfriend.

Which school was that?
Westonbirt School for girls.

And you went straight to the East End? How did you make a living?
I never lived anywhere else. I lived off my boyfriend's student loan for a month and then I got a job working in a shop. Then I started writing for *i-D* and kept writing.

Has writing been your lifelong passion?
Not at school. I just chanced on it. I am doing it until someone catches me out.

Today you are a mover and shaker at the fashion magazine LOVE. *Tell me about style and fashion in this neck of the woods.*
I am more of a wordsmith as opposed to a stylist, so I don't walk down the street and find myself being inspired and influenced. I think it is about the subconscious; I don't know how I am influenced by it. It's like squeezing toothpaste. You just don't know how it's going to get out, but it will get out. I quite like people's nonchalant way of dressing here. I quite like how grubby it is, and I feel very at home. Whereas when I get to West London …

What about West London? Would you move there?
Yes, if you'd buy me a house! But probably not. I want a farm. I would like to live half here and half in the countryside. I don't believe in the middle bit. I don't believe in towns.

Wearing a mottled turquoise Hockley jacket and dress by best friend Mimi Wade, Harriet Verney mucks about with her boyfriend Byron Pritchard, a furniture designer and born-and-bred East Ender (left). **Outside The Society Club on Cheshire Street, Verney has a smoke with the club's founder, Babette Kulik** (opposite).

The avant-garde shop is known for its book launches as well as its collection of twentieth-century first editions and artists' monographs. In the evenings it hosts eclectic poetry readings and alternative literary gatherings. 'It's a great place to feel inspired and meet people,' notes Pritchard

Are you accepted here?
Yeah! I live here. But I actually feel this isn't my *home*. My home is in a field in the countryside; I am more of a tourist here. What really matters is the preservation of the community that we invade. You cannot create that community in a new London tower block like those being built all over the place. That will never have the same feel of community as we do here.

Have you seen a lot of change in the community?
Yes. People love that buzzword *gentrification* quite a lot, but it is also *evolution*, which is very important and bound to happen. If a place stays the same for too long, it will be dull. It has changed, but so have I. What used to excite me about walking down a street that had no lights and illegal bars doesn't excite me as much today! Now I am quite happy to find a Sainsbury's at the end of my road where I can get my Ecover washing-up liquid!

Is part of the attraction of East London its reputation as a creative incubator?
Yes. It can act as a stepping stone. People will see and grab opportunities here and then leave. They don't stay here for long. It's almost like a pinball machine – when you pull it back, it sets off, and then you're off. You go to another part of town or to another city. It's a place that is subliminally governed by the young but actually owned by the old and rich.

Harriet admires the bartender's moves at The Society Club (above)**. Wrapped in a fluffy pink coat** (opposite)**, she heads to Pamela's on Kingsland Road** (right)**. One of the many cocktail bars cropping up between Shoreditch and Dalston, the bar is themed around '90s beach 'babe' Pamela Anderson. Of Kingsland Road, Harriet says, 'It's not a street but rather an area with attitude and a soul of its own'**

'What really matters is the preservation
of the community that we invade'

In 2011, East London councils outlawed the establishment of new strip clubs and sex shops, citing as exceptions such 'well-run, longstanding' establishments as Ye Olde Axe, a combination of traditional pub, strip club and fashionable nightclub. An 1850s Grade II listed building with a Queen Anne-style brick exterior, terracotta lettering, a four-storey turret and its original clock face, Ye Olde Axe is located at the lower end of Hackney Road. The plan of the interior remains intact, featuring the original light fixtures and inlaid cut-glass panels to create private booths

Ye Olde Axe is one of the oldest strip clubs in East London; it's said famously that Sweeney Todd was last seen running up its stairs

DOREEN GOLDING

Pearly Queen of Bow Bells

Doreen Golding (opposite) cites its multicultural heritage as a key to East London's ethos, noting, 'London has always been a hotchpotch of everybody.' Changes around Brick Lane are most apparent through cuisine: 'Traditional food used to be salt-beef bagels; now it's a curry.' Golding's jacket is decorated with badges of charities she has worked with, with a nod to the Pearlies' nineteenth-century heritage. 'We've also kept the style up with the blooms on the ladies' hats and ostrich feathers,' she explains. Pearly King of Woolwich Clive Bennet (standing at the far left) describes the area as the 'centre of the world on a Sunday morning' (below). The Pearlies are a London charitable organisation and regularly spend their Sunday mornings on Brick Lane meeting locals and tourists. Their hand-sewn jackets include life-related symbols. 'The flowers are friendships, the horseshoe for good luck,' Golding explains. 'It's all good-luck signs and the same wherever you go.' The wearing of clothes decorated with 'pearl' (actually mother-of-pearl buttons) is associated with Henry Croft, an early-twentieth-century orphan street sweeper who collected money for charity. At the time, London costermongers (street traders) sported trousers decorated along the seams with pearl buttons that had been found by market traders. Croft adapted this practice to create a pearly suit to draw attention to himself and aid his fundraising activities

How long have you been Pearly Queen?
I've been Queen full-time for twenty years now. My parents were market traders, my husband was a taxi driver, and I'm a freeman of the City of London. That's how I got my title.

How would you define the East today?
It's now an Asian area; prior to that it was a Jewish area; prior to that it was Irish. It's always been immigrants. Most of the old white English, the Pearlies, moved out to Essex, Basildon and Southend.

Do you feel any resentment about that?
No, because this is the Port of London. Everybody comes to London and thinks the streets are paved with gold, and then they find out they're not! My great grandparents were from Poland and Russia, and they lived in Brick Lane. In the 1960s there was a great 'slum' clearance; they knocked down the little terraced houses and rehoused everybody in tower blocks. A lot of us didn't want to stay so we moved out a bit further. It was a good spirit living in little houses; there was more of a community.

Talk to me about the ethos of being a Pearly.
We give our services free to any charity that wants our support. It was founded in late Victorian/early Edwardian times. We've kept the style up, with the blooms on the ladies' hats and ostrich feathers too. Everybody's outfit is different, but we incorporate the traditional signs.

'Everybody comes to London and thinks the streets are paved with gold, and then they find out they're not'

Doreen Golding

VAUXHALL ART CAR BOOT SALE

Running since 2004, the Vauxhall Art Car Boot Sale travels around the UK, with the Old Truman Brewery in East London one of its designated stops. On a day devoted to art, performance and vintage cars, the brewery's courtyard is taken over by a host of established and emerging artists. Founded by Karen Ashton and her sister Helen Hayward, the sale offers a unique opportunity for art lovers to speak directly to artists and acquire exclusive works. Gathering creatives from East London and further afield via recommendations and personalised invitations, participants have included the likes of Tracey Emin, street artist Ben Eine and Sir Peter Blake among a plethora of others, both known and unknown. Artists have their work on display in stalls and sometimes in the backs of vintage cars. Among them might be Polly Morgan, with her contemporary take on taxidermy (above); **Gavin Turk, showing a selection of handmade prints** (opposite, second column, second from the top)**; and Bob and Roberta Smith** (opposite, first column, middle)**, known for his politically charged Pop slogans**

PRINCESS JULIA

Cultural Correspondent, Editor, Model & DJ

Princess Julia ... Do you think of yourself as East End royalty?
Just made it up; it's a case of reinvention.

Tell me about your background.
I was born in Hackney, but I grew up in North London. I'm the daughter of a Hungarian refugee and an English mother who came from Surrey, wherever that is. I'm just like anybody else, curious and inquisitive. Early in the '70s I was looking at magazines and TV. I guess the most pivotal moment for a lot of people of my generation was Ziggy Stardust in 1972 on *Top of the Pops*. When I left home, I became a junior apprentice hairdresser in Knightsbridge and many of the juniors were involved in clubs. It was 1976, right in the middle of the punk scene, and that's how I met a lot of lifelong friends. It was a very small scene, quite gay and very creative.

So you've zigzagged your way through London ...
It's my home city so I like to explore it. I gravitate to the areas where I think the action is. In the late '70s I was part of the New Romantic scene. I met Boy George and we became friends. I lived in a Warren Street squat with Stephen Jones, Kim Bowl, Jeremy Healy and many others. Everyone was a student either at Central Saint Martins or Middlesex. It was the beginning of the Thatcher era and there was a sense of optimism. In the '80s we all got rehoused to so-called 'undesirable' Council flats around the Camden area, which was fantastic. By that point Boy George was on the path to being a pop star, and various people from the Blitz scene like Spandau Ballet, Marc Almond, Gary Numan and all those electro-pop stars got signed. New people were gravitating towards London in the '80s as well as the likes of Leigh Bowery. By the mid-'80s, people were doing their own one-nighter events and becoming quite famous.

East London royalty Princess Julia spins playfully in the quiet of Heneage Street (opposite) **– just behind the hustle and bustle of Brick Lane** (left) **– wearing her sparkly** gauze ASHISH outfit. She has played vital roles on many alternative scenes, beginning in the 1970s and '80s through Blitz and Kinky Gerlinky up to the present moment

Was the London club scene influenced by New York?
Towards '86/7 was my official moment of DJing that carried on through the '90s. I used to go to New York often. There's always been a vibrant conversation between creative people in New York and London. Hopefully it continues if this government doesn't restrict us all.

Did you ever feel restricted as a woman DJ?
I came up in the gay scene, but the club scene opened up globally and I found myself on other scenes too. It didn't really occur to me, at the beginning, that I was pioneering things for womankind. It was only after that question was asked of me that I thought, Okay, I better be serious about this because I have to pave the way for other people. I think boys and their toys like to have an air that it's really complicated to be a DJ, but it's not. It's simple; I blew the lid off that. I also did things other than music. I modelled in Japan and used to worry that I didn't have a focused career. I'm a person that sees creativity as many threads which cross over, more like a tapestry. Now I've realised that was a very modern way of living. I try and approach different things I do with an equal amount of energy and also set myself challenges. That's how I'm now a trained writer, but I write in my chatty way.

How would you like to be remembered?
As desperate like everyone else.

And how would you sum up the East End today?
It's a hive of activity. Everything's in a state of flux, and I think it's kind of interesting, isn't it?

Princess Julia loses herself in her thoughts in a red velvet corner of the two-hundred-year-old pub Pride of Spitalfields. She has lived all over the city but currently calls East London home

'Everything's in a state of flux, and I think it's kind of interesting, isn't it?'

Street art by persons known and unknown graces the walls of Shoreditch beside Truman Brewery (above). Once one of the world's largest breweries, today its 10 acres host a mix of businesses and event spaces. At the junction of Hanbury Street and Brick Lane, Belgian artist ROA created his 12-metre crane (opposite) in honour of East Asian folktales featuring the bird as a symbol of peace, happiness, longevity and wisdom

JOHNNY VERCOUTRE

Founder of Time for Tea

Do you consider yourself a Londoner?
Yes. I was born in Highgate at the Dick Whittington
Hospital so I've always lived in London. I moved to
Shoreditch in the late '90s when it was still quite a slum.
I purchased Time for Tea, which we restored from a
derelict building.

What's the story behind Time for Tea?
It was a house and I lived there. We had a teashop on
the ground floor which also sold vintage design. It used
to be a watchmaker's space in the 1800s. He made the
clock for St Leonard's Church. 'Time for Tea' is also my
philosophy of life! I recently sold the building because it
was in Shoreditch High Street, the trendiest part of town
where all the nightclubs are open till 4.00 a.m. Hackney
Council weren't really bothered about residential noise
and preferred to make money from alcohol sales instead,
so I sold the building.

When did your obsession with the past begin?
I started collecting historic vehicles when I was eighteen
– classic vehicles, old Jeeps – and then I started buying
clothes to go with the vehicles in the '80s.

And what drew you to Shoreditch in the first instance?
It's always been a very good community. When I was a
child, my grandparents brought me here to buy me my
first tortoise because there used to be a pet market in
the '70s and '80s. When I was a teenager, I would go out
partying all night long. Brick Lane was the first place
I came to and got bagels late at night. It was where you'd
come to party. First bagel, first tortoise …

**Johnny Vercoutre outside
Time for Tea** (opposite),
the Georgian townhouse
he bought twenty years
ago on Shoreditch High
Street. Once a branch of
the London Savings Bank,
the building went on to
serve as a clockmaker's
to St Leonard's Church in
Shoreditch, a pawnbroker's
and a stationer's. Vercoutre
reinstated its pre-war
interiors, and the result was
a time-capsule tearoom
from the 1940s which
served as the backdrop for
a number of period dramas
as well as his family home.
Though he sold the building
in 2015 due to rising costs
and increasing noise from
neighbouring clubs, he
still visits occasionally.
'I love history and tradition,'
he says of his 1960s suit
from Hunky Dory Vintage
on Brick Lane, with whose
founder, Ian Bondenham
(left), he likes to chat

I have a hard time imagining you as a hard-core party person!
I used to run clubs more than go to them, like the vaudeville Modern Times Club at the Great Eastern Hotel near Liverpool Street. I used to do a show with Paloma Faith and sing 'My Heart Belongs to Daddy'. Great voice. Later, I did a film premiere party at Claridge's and got her to sing there just before she got famous. I always knew she had it in her.

What is your favourite decade?
Different decades for different subjects. If I could go back to any time in history, it would be the 1951 Festival of Great Britain. Clothes and motorbikes I like from the '30s, and then in furniture, design and architecture, definitely the '60s. Everything I own is pretty much pre-1960s.

So are you still living in a specific decade?
Yes, I've gone forward now to the '60s.

Do you have a tea caddy?
I do. It's from the '70s. I had a '70s Electrolux hoover that broke down a few days ago, but I went on eBay and got two fully restored early '60s ones for £50.

And they work?
Yeah, really well. There's no packaging to waste and they're not ugly-looking. Most modern appliances are so disposable and not very well designed.

The suit you're wearing is '60s, isn't it?
Yes. It's from Hunky Dory Vintage. I bought a lot from the States because it was really affordable there and started collecting a lot of '60s furniture from there as well. I love history and tradition. You can study history your whole life and still never learn about everything.

'You can study history [of the East End] your whole life and still never learn about everything'

Vercoutre has a word with artist Adam Dant and his dog Dr Watson on Club Row (opposite). **'My grandparents brought me here to buy my first tortoise,'** Vercoutre remembers of the street. **'It used to be a pet market.'** He enjoys a strong cuppa (left) **from family-owned Syd's Coffee Stall, the oldest food stall in London, on the corner of Calvert Avenue and Shoreditch High Street** (far left). **Cheryl Diamond serves up loose-leaf tea** (above) **from the mahogany-panelled shack, which has survived both the Second World War and gentrification**

MEI-HUI LIU

Founder of Dumpling Heart Supper Club & Secret Rendez-Vous; Designer for Victim Fashion Street

Were you one of the pioneers of creative East London?
I was here in '99. Before that I was on Portobello Road, where I started my market stall. That's where I met all these incredible, interesting and colourful people like Natacha [Marro] and Noel [Stewart]. In '99, I started at Spitalfields Market every Sunday.

What did you sell?
I made clothes during the week and sold them in the market. I came to the East End and lived off Brick Lane in an architect's house. Sir Richard MacCormac and Jocasta Innes were both artists who moved to the East End in the '60s or '70s at the same time as Gilbert & George. They were some of the first people who inspired me and made me want to move here. Then I started to do a party around Brick Lane.

Tell me about Secret Rendez-Vous.
The idea was that it was a secret. I saw people on the street or in the market and I would invite them to my party. We had no Facebook, no Internet, no email, no telephone; it was all word-of-mouth. You had all these empty warehouses around Brick Lane, and there were clubs that had just started like Great Eastern Dining Room. They gave me space for free and I brought all these cool people together once a month at Secret Rendez-Vous. It wasn't just a party, though. I found photographers, hairdressers, makeup artists and designers who would come and show their work. It was like a pop-up. People started to help each other and build relationships. Many are at the top of their game today!

So you created a close-knit creative community but also had a cultural impact?
At the time I did it for fun and for passion. I didn't think about making money; you just gave each other a common platform. About three or four years ago I brought the whole Secret Rendez-Vous to Taiwan and it became a hugely successful project called 'East to East'. I also went to Paris and Rome, but when I came back to London, I realised how different London people are – open-minded, with their own unique style. That's why I decided to stay.

Mei-Hui Liu in her pop-up Dumpling Heart eatery on Calvert Avenue (opposite)**; the wallpaper backdrop features one of her designs. Her dress is one of her own romantic vintage-style creations, paired with shoes by Natacha Marro which she says she 'cannot live without'. One of Britain's first ethical brands, Liu's designs embody frills and frocks made from recycled and sustainable materials. Dumpling Heart, a Taiwanese-style pop-up** (below)**, travels across East London, often presenting salon-style festivities that mix the culinary, art and fashion worlds**

Now you are a jack-of-all-trades with your pop-up Dumpling Heart Supper Club …
That is a new Secret Rendez-Vous, this time with food. I do studio launches for art, fashion and events, all related to people from the old days, like a salon.

The East has changed a lot since the '90s when you first came. Are you still just as enamoured with it?
Everywhere I go, I still want to come back here. Maybe not Brick Lane or Redchurch Street anymore, but it's all still very special. The whole magic of Rendez-Vous is that I created a platform for myself and for other people; it gave lots of people, including myself, confidence to become role models for others and have an opportunity to shine.

'Everywhere I go I still want to come back here'

Mei-Hui Liu in the Cleve Courtyard behind Calvert Avenue (opposite), where she regularly hosts her creative parties, events and fashion shows. Sitting outside her studio-cum-showroom, she samples a batch of 'lace' dumplings (above). Filled with treasures, the space is vintage bric-a-brac heaven, with Victorian cabinets, haberdashery, lace, fabrics, ceramics and other *objets* (left). 'I hope to one day create a museum,' Liu laughs

HASSAN HAJJAJ

Artist & Designer

Hassan Hajjaj in his shop on Calvert Avenue (below), named after the city of his birth, Larache. Packed with recycled lanterns, clothing and baskets (opposite), the shop sources its offerings directly from Morocco and echoes many of the themes found in Hajjaj's diverse artistic practice. Influenced by both his North African heritage and London's club, hip-hop and reggae scenes, Hajjaj moved to East London in the early 1990s. 'The people here have the taste of London, what London's about: music, fashion, the whole lifestyle'

How long you have been operating in this part of the world?
The first time I lived here was 1990; I had a warehouse place till 1996. I moved back in 2005.

What changes have you seen?
London every now and then has a moment. It was Portobello Market in the '60s in West London, Camden in the 1980s, but East London has become the hub of London, the *real* London. There will be another area later that will become the hub of London. I've seen the East morph from a proper neighbourhood to a central part of the world.

Why did you choose to live here?
Economy, to be honest. I came here because I was looking for a place to live and everywhere in London was expensive. Margaret Thatcher was in, recession hit, and with all these empty warehouses, if you smashed all the windows, they were half the rates. So they started renting them. It was the first time they had permission from the Council to be able to live in these spaces. It was a cheap place to rent, and you're like ten minutes from Central London, so it made sense.

If you had to define East London, what aspects distinguish it from other parts of the city?
The people have the taste of London, what London's about – music, fashion, lifestyle.

Do you have any special memories?
Lots of parties back in the day. Bruno's, where you had drum and bass, and we had Björk, MIA – a real underground.

What about Hoxton Square?
When I moved there, there was one café that was kind of trendy. That was the only place you would go to in the whole area. Now you can imagine how many thousands of restaurants there are. You've got to remember it's one of the biggest Council-flat areas in England, and then they had all these new, trendy people moving in in the '80s in these loft spaces, so lots of contrast between working people and these trendy people. It was a bit of an uncomfortable moment, and then it kind of grew together. The younger generation grew up with the trendy people, and the trendy people grew up with the working class, and it became one.

Hajjaj (above) **outside his shop, in front of which he arranges most of his photo shoots. A self-taught artist, he creates studio portraits of friends, musicians and artists, as well as of strangers in Marrakech, often wearing clothes he has designed. His portraits, which combine the vocabularies of fashion photography and Pop art, dot the shop** (opposite) **alongside Morocco-sourced Coca-Cola crates converted into unique design pieces as a comment on branding and the effects of global capitalism**

I remember someone saying that before White Cube moved in, the square had syringes everywhere. Was it very druggy?
Yeah, it was quite rugged. People would smoke or whatever, and then you had working-class men selling Ecstasy to the trendy people. It took a while to find a medium, and then it grew from there, because there was just a couple of offices and a café. That's it. Now it seems to be a safe place.

You are Moroccan by origin and your art is influenced by Moroccan culture. Has it been easy for you to integrate in the East End?
Yes, as I feel I'm a Londoner as much as being Moroccan. (But I don't see myself as being British!)

I see a strong urban influence and colour in your work. Does the East End inform your art at all?
Very much so, as I do lots of my shoots on Calvert Avenue, right outside my shop/studio.

'The younger generation grew up with the trendy people, and the trendy people grew up with the working class, and it became one'

'WE LOOK OUT FOR EACH OTHER HERE. I WANT TO WORK WITH LIKE-MINDED PEOPLE IN THE AREA AND SUPPORT THEIR BUSINESSES AND ACTIVITIES, LIKE LEILA'S ON CALVERT AVENUE'

**MAUREEN PALEY,
GALLERIST**

Colourful fruits and vegetables are displayed beneath posters protesting East End developments at Leila's Shop on Calvert Avenue off Arnold Circus. A beloved local grocer's and café founded by Leila McAlister, Leila's serves fresh seasonal food and encourages returning customers to hang their Barn the Spoon wooden utensils along the wall. Regulars have included artist Leon Kossoff and actress Julie Christie

JOHN DOLAN

Artist

Talk to me about the streets of East London.
I used to sit on Shoreditch High Street, regular as clockwork. When I was homeless, the streets of Islington were where my friends would see me so I went to Shoreditch or Whitechapel and Aldgate East. I found this abandoned car once opposite Spitalfields Church. You couldn't see through the windows and you'd have to scratch away at the dirt to see inside. I lived in that car for six months. I've also lived on the street itself, in doorways and in sleeping bags. It was mad, it was lonely, it was sometimes fun. I used to shoplift; I was a bit of a criminal. Eventually I was living in temporary accommodation until I got rehoused into Shoreditch. Now I live in the Boundary, the oldest estate in Europe.

How did your adventure in painting begin?
I've always been able to draw. My grandfather was a great artist; that's where I get it from. My inspiration is, to begin with, my dog. I started drawing buildings because I liked the look of the old, decrepit buildings in the area. I was using buildings opposite from where I sat in the high street as a study. I must have built and rebuilt these buildings three thousand times in my head and on canvas! I've sold every picture to passers-by.

Tell me about George, your dog, your raison d'être ...
I rescued George and took him on a whim. The next morning I woke up, buried my head in my hands and thought, What have I done? I can just about look after myself, let alone an animal?!

Throughout your life, would you say that art was a companion?
It saved me. It still does save me, every day. I don't need to worry about the roof over my head any more because of art. I also feel more part of the community. I had no identity up until this art stuff happened.

What about your fit in the community going forward?
I will die here in Shoreditch. I'm part of the brickwork as much as the buildings are. I think my story gives people inspiration, especially the young. They see that they don't have to be drug dealers to make money. You only get out of life what you put in. It took me a long while to realise this.

Tell me about your connection to the commercial art world.
I sell on the street, but I also sell through two local galleries: Griffin and Pure Evil. I have worked with the Museum of London and done a project in Southwark Cathedral. Right now, I'm doing a project with *The Big Issue*. And then there's my book, *John and George: The Dog Who Changed My Life*.

What about community work?
My last project was with the Street Leak app. Say you see a homeless person on the street and you want to help them, but you don't want to engage with them. You can alert the charity through the app. The street helped me. It is my turn to help back.

One of London's first housing estates, the Boundary Estate (left), which radiates out from Arnold Circus, was built in 1890 on a mound of rubble from the levelling of London's most notorious Victorian slum, a warren of streets full of disease, prostitutes and thieves. Resident John Dolan spent decades on the street and in and out of prison before finding a reason to give up crime in the form of a Staffordshire terrier (opposite) named George, whom he acquired for the price of a can of lager. Inspired to stay out of trouble, Dolan began to draw on the streets. He often sits and sketches on the bandstand at the centre of Arnold Circus

'The street helped me. It is my turn to help back'

ROCHELLE CANTEEN

Restaurant by Melanie Arnold & Margot Henderson

(top) **Guests celebrating Creative Director Sara Blonstein's birthday include Film Director Harvey Bertram-Brown** (above, right to left) **stylist Karen Binns, The House of Fairy Tales founder Deborah Curtis, Andrea Brown (Blonstein's mother), Rochelle Canteen founder Melanie Arnold and Blonstein's son Sonny**

(right) **Rochelle Canteen founders Melanie Arnold and Margot Henderson enjoy a tipple with the ICA's Executive Director Gregor Muir in the sunny grounds of Rochelle**

(above) **Friends and family of Sara Blonstein gather in the floral courtyard of Rochelle Canteen. In 2004, chefs Melanie Arnold and Margot Henderson created the canteen in a former bike shed on the grounds of Rochelle School, a Victorian building now home to artists and arts organisations. 'We want people to eat here every day,' explains Henderson, 'because you can. Some fancy restaurants you have to lie down after'**

'It's a secret place, and everyone feels that they can do what they like; it's a bit like being at someone's house'

Melanie Arnold

HARVEY BERTRAM-BROWN

Film Director, Creative Director, Art Director & Set Designer

This house used to be a factory, didn't it?
A knicker factory, darling! The neighbourhood is crazy secure, more than anywhere we've lived before.

You are a jack-of-all-creative-trades. From music, to film, to music videos, to retail windows, from New York to London, the lines all blur.
Definitely. I don't like to be called a jack-of-all-trades, though, because the next sentence is 'master of none', and I'd like to think I'm master of all trades. My passion is fashion. When I was doing my degree at the Royal College of Art, I realised that fashion is bigger than the rag trade. There's another side to it that is intangible, the zeitgeist of a moment. These days fashion is about lifestyle; there aren't any boundaries. Film-making means that I'm involved not only in clothes but also with context. I choose models, music, the environment, the set, the dialogue. I'm involved in so many things because for me they all encompass fashion.

How does the East End inform your thinking?
I find inspiration everywhere, but it felt like we were fish out of water in Hampstead. When I first moved there, it had this idea of the artisan, the craftsman. With time, the artisans seemed to be gazumped by Gap and Starbucks. We definitely didn't belong there, so we came to the East End, where we rub shoulders with more of our kind. There's interesting spaces with interesting people doing interesting things. Everybody seems to be open-minded here, with a smile on their face. In the West End, if you smile, people hold their bags a bit tighter.

Harvey Bertram-Brown and his husband Steve Riseley have lived in a converted knicker factory near Spitalfields since 2013 (left)**. Thinking of moving from Hampstead, Bertram-Brown was walking round the area when he came upon Tracey Emin's neon sign outside The Golden Heart that read 'Sandra and Dennis, 35 years' – referring to the iconic pub's** landlords, Sandra and Dennis Esquilant. As his deceased parents were also called Sandra and Dennis, Bertram-Brown (opposite) took the coincidence as a sign 'from above': 'Whatever it took, we had to live here, it was made for us. It was one of those drop-dead moments in your life where you know what you have to do!'

Bertram-Brown (left) walks Calvin Street, outside his home in East London. 'We've got a big community on this street and we're friends with all our neighbours' he explains. Bertram-Brown employed local architect Chris Dyson – known for many sensitive historic conservation projects in Shoreditch – to create his apartment, mixing stripped-back minimalism with glamorous accents; he describes the glass office and concrete floor as 'very us' (opposite). The 1901 Bechstein piano represents both an investment to facilitate the writing of some of his musicals and to encourage Steven (Bertram-Brown's partner Steven Riseley, pictured right) to practise his playing. 'It's like learning to drive on a Porsche,' Bertram-Brown jokes. 'Even the noises you make sound fantastic, especially given the acoustics in the apartment.' The place feels like 'the eye of the storm' at the heart of the area's rough edges, he adds. 'We sleep with our windows open and a sense of something green around us'

Would you call yourself an optimist?
Definitely. I've been so blessed the last couple of years because I've been rewarded in what I do creatively and I've found the love of my life after thinking I might be alone forever. Though everything can change in a heartbeat, for the moment I feel secure, and that helps you be optimistic and embrace life.

What role does creativity play in your well-being?
I'm not shy to say something, and in my line of work I'm allowed to say something about things which I find interesting. The first day I woke up in this house, I sat down at my desk, locked myself in my little glass box for three days and wrote *Blue Jeans* [the musical] straight through, the whole thing in three days. The film has got some real magic to it because it's autobiographical, albeit dressed up in a beautiful allegorical tale. A lot of people seem to identify with it, so it feels like it has the potential to appeal to a huge audience.

'There's interesting spaces with interesting people doing interesting things. Everybody seems to be open-minded here, with a smile on their face'

LAVINIA

Drag Queen, Actor, Singer & Dancer

What was it like growing up in the East End?
I was born in the '50s at Hackney Hospital. I lived in Navarino Mansions in Dalston Lane, which was built by the Four Per Cent Industrial Dwellings Company. It was built for Jewish immigrants from Eastern Europe and has been part of Hackney's character ever since. There were about 320 flats so although I went to Stamford Hill's Catholic school, I grew up with loads of Jewish people. My dad was a porter, so often I would go into the homes and meet people and they'd know me. He'd be decorating so I'd see the insides of these glamorously decorated 1930s houses. Growing up, Hackney was full of small industries and green spaces. We'd go to all the different parks like Hackney Downs. Mare Street was where the entertainment was. I remember the early '50s with the Yiddish Theatre, and the Regal cinema that is now a Sainsbury's. And lots of prostitution.

Fast forward to New York in the '80s …
I did go back and forth with a show called the BLOOLIPS, a gay-theatre drag troupe. So I did experience New York from the late '70s into the '90s.

What brought you back to London?
Hackney did, because luckily I maintained my little flat here. America is a hard, tough place to live. I wasn't rich, but we had a healthcare and social-welfare state in the UK which made it easier to live. That said, I've done a lot of travelling and there will be more.

How would you differentiate Hackney from the rest of London?
It used to be that everyone would go west; now it's from the centre going out. Hackney is incredibly multi-dimensional ethnically. This has changed London in the last ten to fifteen years. You can't afford to live here any more. People have moved to Walthamstow and they're bussed into work. East London has gone upmarket, but when it's full of luxury apartments, it won't have the same flavour as it once did.

Lavinia holds an Orpheum Theatre (New York) poster advertising the BLOOLIPS (opposite)**, the gay theatre troupe in which he featured for nearly twenty years. 'We were all radical fairies at the time,' he says. Now semi-retired, Lavinia spends time** **archiving old material at home in Navarino Mansions, Dalston, and in drag at the occasional evening event** (left)**. 'I'm white, working class, male, gay, a drag queen, actor, singer, dancer and born in Hackney,'** **winks Lavinia**

Tell me about the role you've played in the LGBTQ movement.

Back in 1971, when gay liberation was happening, we were all radical fairies in a way. We weren't calling ourselves that, and there were different kinds – political kinds, straight, liberal kinds, the beginning of the butch, the beginning of the clone. But in 1976/7, it was as if the hippy thing allowed you to be androgynous. We started coming out of the closet and into the clubs and bars. BLOOLIPS came about as we wanted to put drag in front of people, not just making a statement on the street – street theatre almost. Onstage, you have more space to get ideas across. Saying that, it's hard to walk around in drag. I can't believe the youngsters today, but they've always been like that – they're fearless! When I was in New York, there were a lot of connections between East London and New York, with Jonny Woo living in my flat. I was able to inspire the drags in London to go to New York because I was there. I was able to help other drag artists make that break.

So people followed in your footsteps?

Everyone is unique, each face is different, and the acts change. I was lucky enough to bump into Jonny Woo and was inspired that this nutcase could roll into a bar and cheer everyone up.

Is there a difference in the drag scenes in East London and New York?

Many drag queens I met in New York had a different sophistication, a different realness. East London has a rougher edge. People call it 'East End Drag' because they wear beards and eye makeup. This was reminiscent of old radical drags that had beards and lipstick, or a handbag and brooch. There's different types of drag in both scenes: low drag, which is just the handbag or lips, then middle drag, which is the full face, and then high drag, which is what I turn up like.

Are you still an active drag artist?

I'm active but on sabbatical. I'm archiving my old material from BLOOLIPS at the moment and teaching Alexander Technique. I still learn songs but more for myself. I've done a lot of stuff, about forty years of acting, doing, singing, dancing and the gay thing. I've made my living through performing. The next thirty years I'm going to be more spiritual, not up on stage. It's good to take a step back as I've done everything – cleaning, shop windows, bars, prop-making, costume-making, every job I could lay my hands on. Even woodwork and furniture-making!

Lavinia scans the frontage of the Hackney Empire (above) **on Mare Street, where he used to perform and serve interval drinks at the bar. 'Sometimes you just have to do what you can to pay the rent,' he observes**

'**Mare Street was where the entertainment was. I remember the early '50s with the Yiddish Theatre, and the Regal cinema that is now a Sainsbury's**'

HACKNEY EMPIRE

East London's iconic music hall-turned-variety theatre has hosted stars from Charlie Chaplin to Jennifer Saunders and Dawn French. Built in 1901 by Frank Matcham, the Empire has passed through many different hands over the years. Once threatened with demolition, in 2001 it had a £17 million refurbishment and has since returned to life as East London's theatrical base, embracing a local and global community of artists and audiences

PHILIP ILSON

Director of the London Short Film Festival

Why do short films fascinate you?
My interest began when I made films in the '90s and showed them at a South London festival, Exploding Cinema. You turned up with a video or a reel of film and screened it yourself, away from the upper echelons of the film industry. I then started a club, the Halloween Society, which ultimately became the London Short Film Festival.

How varied is your festival?
We screen all types of film. The bulk are British, but we are open to international submissions. We show about 350 shorts and do events all year.

How has the film scene changed since the '90s?
There were lots of underground and alternative club nights, such as Off Centre (run by Neil Boorman and Ross Clarke) and Onyx (run by Steven Eastwood), which combined performance art, video art and experimental music. Unfortunately, the scene was unsustainable in terms of budget. People didn't notice what was happening at the grassroots level back then; we even picketed the press launch of BFI London Film Festival in Leicester Square because of the funding shortage. There's no longer an alternative or underground feeling to these events.

What has survived of those subcultures?
Shooting People, set up in the '90s, is a networking website for film-makers; they are still based in Hoxton Street. Lux started as the London Film-makers' Co-op in the '60s and in the late '90s got Lottery funding to build premises in Hoxton Square, but they only lasted two years. They moved to Shacklewell Lane (which used to be nicknamed 'Crackwell Lane') and are still there. It's mental if you look at Shoreditch now; you can't imagine having those spaces for performance art on a Saturday night.

Philip Ilson grabs a coffee at Mouse & de Lotz on Shacklewell Lane (opposite). Understanding the changes in East London through his parents' stories and born on the Isle of Dogs pre-1960s 'when it was definitely not an area you wanted to live,' he comments, 'Mum does laugh when I say we were having drinks on the canal like in Venice; she can't believe that.' 'Away from the upper echelons of the film industry' is how Ilson imagined his first events in the 1990s. He holds his open-submission short-film festival at Hackney Picturehouse (left), a core venue due to the concentration of youth and film-makers in the area

SOPHIE PARKIN

Writer, Artist, Actor & Founder of Vout-O-Reenee's

Tell me about Vout-O-Reenee's.
Vout-O-Reenee's is an arts club in Prescot Street, in the crypt of the Roman Catholic Church of the English Martyrs. So we're on hallowed ground. The church is community-minded, and they like the idea that we've brought the artist community here. The name is a reference to somebody who should be remembered: a handsome American jazz star called Slim Gaillard who was known as 'Dark Gable'. He invented the language Vout-O-Reenee, a dictionary of jive slang. In *On the Road*, Jack Kerouac and the beatniks are going to see Slim Gaillard; that's why they are speaking the way they do. It's actually Vout.

What about the space, the decor, the design references?
I've had eight different artists paint the floors, the walls and the ceilings. The hallway is based on a design of the Givenchy building in the 1930s done by Christian Bérard, who was the Art Director on all the Jean Cocteau films. It's an homage to *La Belle et la bête*. We have a sculpture by Andrew Logan, who was part of the original East End. He was in one of the great warehouses in Wapping and then his studio burned down. He did the first Alternative Miss World. The ethics of this club are based on those of The Colony Room: 'Leave your egos outside on the doormat, please.'

You are not from the East End, or are you?
I'm London-bred, but I was born in Chelsea. I moved to the East End when I was eighteen, when I was at Saint Martins. I was living in Hackney and then moved back here to have my children in about '86. I've been around the East End for a long time.

Sophie Parkin at her private members' club 'for the surrealistically distinguished', Vout-O-Reenee's, intended as a revival of earlier clubs dedicated to emerging young artists (opposite). A former head of performance at Chelsea Arts Club, Parkin gravitated naturally to East London and believes that meeting points like Vout-O-Reenee's help to promote, demonstrate and exhibit members' work (left). 'Fifty per cent of being an artist is the conversation you have with your audience,' she explains. 'This doesn't happen if you just sit alone.' More generally, she sees social hubs like hers as 'a way of defining the life of the place, because people are interested in getting together and socialising, and when the pubs start closing down you have to be frightened. The soul goes out, and you can't get it back once it's gone'

You experienced Soho in its heyday, didn't you?

Well, Soho has become like Covent Garden. It changed from being aristocratic and French to democratic – world citizens and nobody speaking the same language – to the language of advertising in the '60s and '70s, to film in the '80s, and now it's become the language of tourism. Nobody wants to believe that you're at the end of an era, and that what was so glorious about Soho will be lost forever. It always was a large, involuntary space. Post-war, there were five hundred clubs in that square mile. Now there's only five, at best. Clubs are a way of defining the life of a place, because people are interested in getting together and socialising. When the pubs start closing down, you have to be frightened. The soul goes out. You've got to protect against the big brands coming in. People in the East End are very protective, but they're still creeping in.

Has the East End retained its identity?

The East End is still very multicultural. I feel we should welcome everybody. It makes it into a richer society, and people who come to new countries try harder. Us lazy sods who've been here for ages never make anything happen! In my club, I am trying to congregate like-minded souls who aren't interested in taking vast amounts of drugs and place them in a social non-egotistical atmosphere.

How did the club come about?

I really wasn't focused on opening a club in the East End when I moved here. I wrote a book on the sixty-year history of The Colony Room and everybody kept saying to me, 'Where's our Colony Room now?' I thought, Well, maybe that's what I should do now! From the moment I walked into this place, I felt the vibe. But I first had to convince the priest!

And you did …

Now we're firm friends. We do lots of music, spoken word, poetry, performance art, theatre, dance, exhibitions and cinema. What I want is good conversation leading to creativity. Creativity doesn't happen in a vacuum. It needs other things in order for it to thrive, like bacteria. It needs the right atmosphere. An artist came in here last night and she's done all this amazing work, but she doesn't want to expose it. I told her that 50 per cent of being an artist is the conversation you have with your audience. It's the same with writing. Everyone can write away in their bedroom, but it takes balls to go out there and publish. If you're really lucky, you'll find an agent and you'll be swimmingly going forwards.

Sophie outside the Roman Catholic Church of the English Martyrs on Prescot Street, designed by Augustus Pugin, a Gothic Revival architect who worked on the interior of the Palace of Westminster (opposite)**. Daughter of novelist Molly Parkin, Sophie grew up among bohemian royalty and as a student hung out alongside Francis Bacon and Lucian Freud at The Colony Room in Dean Street. The ethics of Vout-O-Reenee's echo the Soho artist-driven members' clubs of the 1980s. As Parkin explains, 'What I am trying to do with the club is congregate like-minded souls who aren't interested in taking vast amounts of drugs in order to be in a social atmosphere and aren't interested in their own egos.' The eclectic decor of her club includes retro toilets** (below)**, as well as design input from interior designer Susan Dalgleish (layout), Oriel Harwood (light fittings) and Monet experts Morgan Paton and Brian Barnes (garden-room decor)**

'Creativity doesn't happen in a vacuum. It needs other things in order for it to thrive, like bacteria'

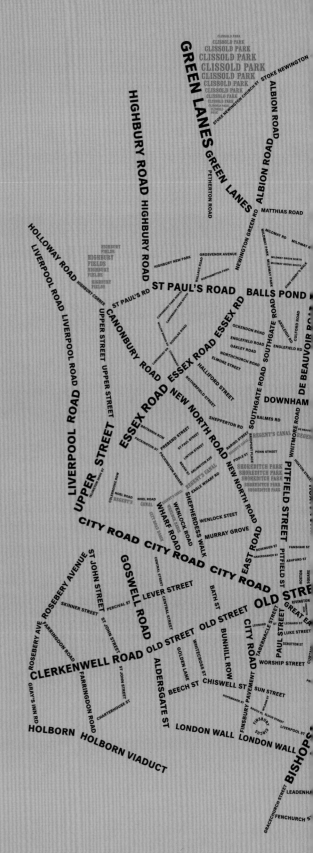

WHITECHAPEL BELL FOUNDRY

'Two sticks and an apple'
say the bells of Whitechapel

The Whitechapel Bell Foundry, possibly the world's most famous bell foundry, was established in 1570. It produced the bells of Big Ben, the original Liberty Bell ordered by the Superintendents of Pennsylvania in 1751, and the peal of bells which rang on the Herald Barge for the Queen's Diamond Jubilee River Pageant, among many others. Owned by the Hughes family since 1904, the foundry moved to Smithfield in 2017 due to the high cost of maintaining the Grade II listed building in Whitechapel. Noting that the demand for church bells has declined year on year while the costs of employment and keeping up with manufacturing legislation and insurance have continued to rise, the family donated their last cast bell and archive to the Museum of London

Artist Duo

Nikki Bell and Ben
Langlands (opposite) in the
first-floor space of their
studio. *Frozen Sky* (1999),
a digitally controlled neon
sculpture composed of
international airport codes,
hangs in the background,
while *Interlocking Chair*
(1989) provides seating
and references the
duo's 'balancing and
interchange' over their
forty-year collaboration.

'Our relationship is
symmetrical, but in other
ways we're very different
people,' explains Langlands.
Having acquired the derelict
four-storey Whitechapel
building in 1982, Langlands
& Bell transformed it into a
minimalist space, with the
exception of their wood-
clad oval bathroom (above),
co-designed with Ashley
Hicks and replete with
a secret door

*Would it be fair to say that you are East London
pioneers?*
Langlands: We used to come here a lot in the '70s and
'80s to Brick Lane Market, Club Row. The market was
a bigger social and economic event in those days, before
shopping malls. Whole generations of families would
go there together. There was a real mix of cultures:
Bangladeshi, Jewish, Maltese, West Indian, Chinese. We
also used to go to the East End to eat, because the food
was very good and inexpensive. We moved here in 1980
from North London.
Bell: There were also lots of abandoned buildings. We
loved exploring them, their histories and wonderful rich
diversity. Many were completely empty; you could just
open a broken door and walk through.
    One of our first installations was *Traces of Living* for
Interim Art, the gallery in Maureen Paley's house. We
made a series of white tables and chairs with glass tops
and filled them with East End found objects displayed like
museum artefacts through which art could be discussed
– from a hand-carved rolling pin to a stock brick, a dried
rat and a dried cauliflower from the market. We were
fascinated with layering old and new.
Langlands: This layering of history happens everywhere
but was more evident here for two reasons. One: There
were more cultures continually arriving and living side by
side, and that had been going on for three hundred years,
since the area had begun to urbanise with the expansion
of the docks. Two: The layers were more evident here.
They'd had pockets of wealth in the seventeenth and early
eighteenth centuries, but then the economy collapsed so
people couldn't afford to rebuild. Things were just left, so
there was lots of fascinating domestic architecture from
the eighteenth century. When we came here, the Georgian
houses in Spitalfields were sweatshops full of sewing
machines. No hot water, outside toilets. Now they're
residential again.

What about this particular house?
Bell: It has lots of histories, including a famous murder
that occurred here in 1874: the brush-maker Henry
Wainwright murdered his mistress Harriet Lane and
buried her under the floor. Everyone laughed at us –
the building was full of pigeons and in such a decrepit
state – but we had practical experience that we applied
to renovating it.

Langlands & Bell outside their studio (above), **previously a belt factory, a Christmas-cracker factory, the annex to a synagogue and a brush-maker's workshop where Henry Wainwright notoriously murdered his mistress in 1874 and buried her under the floorboards. Although they did most of the renovation themselves over an eighteen-month period,** they found no trace of her. 'One of our fascinations has always been exploring the histories and wonderful, rich diversity of these buildings,' explains Bell. Though the East End has been heavily redeveloped since they first arrived in the area, the artists remain dedicated to exploring Whitechapel (opposite), **even if they now view East London through novel lenses**

How did the area change in the '90s?
Langlands: The YBAs were beginning to move in: Tim Noble, Sue Webster, Gary Hume, Tracey Emin. That added another layer. When we first came here, there were still bomb sites and many derelict buildings. In a very short time, every bomb site was developed and every building was restored or converted. The traditional rag trade and shoe trade moved out to the peripheries.

Would you say that the East End is still rich in spirit and content?
Langlands: It's still more interesting than anywhere else in London, but it's very different from when we first came. Back then, it was a revelation, full of mystery, full of social history. Space was cheaper, materials were cheaper, clothes were cheaper, food was cheaper. When you're an artist with virtually no income, that's very important. It's no longer like that, but it's still great in many ways. The food's still good and the people are far more interesting than anywhere else in London. But it somehow lacks some of that deep, rich texture it once had.
Bell: All the characters have now died. There was an extraordinary old boy, a rag-and-bone man living in a caravan with dogs and cats, and a lady who ran a pub who lowered a basket on a rope every morning wearing her bra. And Mr Clean – a crazy tramp who swept the street with a dust-pan and brush – he put bread and butter in the basket for her, and was allowed to keep the change to buy curry from the Indian down the road.
Langlands: And then the history around here! Look at Tower House. When Stalin came to London for the 5th Congress of Russia's Communist Party, this is where he stayed. So did George Orwell when he was writing *Down and Out in Paris and London* and Jack London when he wrote *The People of the Abyss*.

What about the connection between the two of you? How does it work?
Bell: Art is about relationships. The way we balance the interchange and flow is part of our relationship. In our work, symmetry is important, but disrupting it is equally important.

'Back then ... space was cheaper, materials were cheaper, clothes were cheaper, food was cheaper. When you're an artist with virtually no income, that's very important'

IWONA BLAZWICK

Director of the Whitechapel Gallery

Talk to me about your relationship with the Whitechapel Gallery.

I have been at the Whitechapel Gallery for fourteen years. My first visit was in 1979 as a student. I saw *Eva Hesse* and it blew me away. I knew then that contemporary art was going to be important for my life. In the '80s and '90s, the Tate was not known for being ultra-contemporary so the ICA, the Whitechapel Gallery and the Hayward were hugely influential. Every important artist I knew would come to Whitechapel. There have also been pioneering curators at both Chisenhale and the Showroom. These programmes were laboratories showing the next thing. The first time I saw Rachel Whiteread's work was when she made *Ghost* and cast an entire room at Chisenhale. So the East End was *the* place you had to go to.

You live and work in the East End. Talk to me about the community.

The area is diverse and cosmopolitan. It has always welcomed exiles from other countries. It started with Germany in the sixteenth century, the Huguenots from France in the seventeenth and eighteenth centuries, and then in the nineteenth century, because of anti-Semitism in Eastern Europe, an influx from the Eastern European Jewish community, Austria and Germany. In the 1950s, it switched to welcoming an Asian community from South Asia, India, Pakistan and Bangladesh. Every wave has left its mark on architecture, cuisine and the area's ethos. One of the most potent changes was a Huguenot chapel that became a Jewish synagogue and is now a mosque. Because it's also outside the official city walls, it has been a place for the dispossessed, the exiled and the avant-garde.

Why has the area been a hotbed of avant-garde thinking?

It partly stems from being excluded. If you think, I can't be part of the past, it follows that 'I'm going to shape the future.' So this place has been associated with new ideas, particularly regarding aesthetics and literature. It's also to do with the demise of industry. It was a working-class area for docking and shipping, but the docks closed and all the warehouses and factories gradually became derelict. In the 1960s, Dominic Harvey and David Pantone were desperate for space and formed Acme. Then Bridget [Riley] with two other artists formed SPACE. Acme found liveable workspace in Beck Road which was all derelict workers' cottages. They went to Hackney Council to ask if they could renovate them and have the whole street for

Iwona Blazwick in front of German artist Thomas Ruff's 2007 camera-less photograph *Substrat 34 I* (opposite) at the Whitechapel's *Electronic Superhighway* exhibition (2016). London's first publicly funded gallery for temporary exhibitions, the Whitechapel opened in 1901. 'One of the hallmarks of its founders,' explains Blazwick, 'is to never patronise the audience. They have always been committed to that which is most interesting, most radical and most significant.' Built by Charles Harrison Townsend, an adherent to the Arts and Crafts Movement, the gallery features street-level access and natural light in the foyer and top gallery. Blazwick oversaw the 2009 extension that joined the building with the iconic Passmore Edwards Library, thus creating further studio rooms and exhibition spaces. Artist Rachel Whiteread installed *Tree of Life* (2012), a series of cast-bronze and gilt leaves, across the façade (below)

a peppercorn rent. Hackney Council agreed, and all these artists renovated these places which until then had been filled with garbage and dead pigeons. Maureen Paley was one of those people. It's a testament to how good artists are at making something out of nothing, using their skills to make liveable workspace. I think cheap rents, a climate of experimental interpretation and outsider-ness are key ingredients in the mix.

As Director of the Whitechapel Gallery, do you feel a sense of responsibility to your community?
The gallery was founded on a mission to bring great art to the people of the East End and the world. One of the hallmarks of its founders and its directors has been to never patronise the audience. The very first show in 1901 attracted 260,000 people, mostly illiterate. The gallery was also the first place to show Picasso, the first place to show Mark Rothko, and on and on. Today, there are special programmes collaborating with primary school kids. We have family days which are packed with the local community. We've been working with twenty or thirty local Asian women as part of the City Gateways programme to get them to speak English and feel confident. It's about mutual exchange and respect. We also have groups that work with the homeless, people with disabilities and young families. We have an amazing youth group called Duchamp & Sons which is composed of local kids aged fifteen to twenty-two. One of the attractions is food; many teens come as it doesn't involve spending money. We're trying to offer a warm, dry place where they can come and do something creative. They are our ambassadors because they network like crazy and bring their mates. We're always trying to think about barriers and how we can remove them.

How do you see your future?
Before 2009, we were a *Kunsthalle* and now we're a museum. We make career surveys, dramatic shows, and we commission new work, as well as hosting guest collections that would otherwise sit in storage. We also have our archive shows which display recent history. We recently started work with a consortium of fifteen partners around the world, all with a black-box space for moving-image work. From Texas to Afghanistan, Istanbul and Russia, each local curator nominates one moving-image artist and everyone in the consortium shows it. That is the future: global co-operation, global awareness and using platforms to show local artists in a space for freedom of expression and creativity.

'Every artist I knew would come here,' remembers Blazwick of Whitechapel Gallery in the late '70s and early '80s. The cantilevered stone staircase, which originally led to the old children's library (opposite), now connects with the new study rooms and exhibition spaces. 'Its mission,' explains Blazwick of the gallery (above), 'was always to bring great art to the people of the East End'

'Every wave has left its mark on architecture, cuisine and the area's ethos. One of the most potent changes was a Huguenot chapel that became a Jewish synagogue and is now a mosque'

SARA BLONSTEIN

**Creative Director of a fashion event
& production agency**

Creative maven Sara
Blonstein at ease in her
East End home (opposite),
encircled by designer furs,
bags and clothes from her
dressing room. Founder
of Blonstein Creative
Production, the fashion-
scene mainstay has worked
with clients ranging from
Roksanda Ilincic, Vivienne
Westwood and Gareth Pugh
to Lancôme, Selfridges and
Absolut. Wearing a vintage
Emilio Pucci cape (below),
Blonstein scans the canal
outside her home. 'This is
Palm Springs-meets-East
Hackney,' she quips, 'which
is kind of my life'

Where are you from originally?
I am from Wimbledon, West London. My Jewish family
originally came to the East End from Russia and Poland
in 1890. My grandmother's father started a famous shoe
business in Whitechapel; they were the first to import
Italian shoes. But they all moved out because they
thought the East End was too poor. I first moved here
in 1997 with my boyfriend. We saw old Nevio Pellicci
(known as Neville to his East End buddies) sitting on
the front step of his house, in the sun. We said, 'Do you
know anything that is for sale?' He said, 'Jo just died.
Five doors down. Put a note in the door.' So we did, and
they contacted us. Before that, I used to come to East
London in the late '80s and early '90s, and we would go to
Brick Lane on Sunday morning for the massive antique
bric-a-brac. It was still like it had been, bombed from the
war. We knew everyone and used to go to the bagel shop.
I always had this love affair with the area. Now, I am
here on Chisenhale Road on Hertford Union Canal with
my backdrop as Victoria Park. I call it 'yummy mummy'
territory even though that's not quite so because we've
got the Chisenhale Gallery next door.

The fun-loving Blonstein can't fail to be noticed in her leopard-print Volkswagen Beetle (above). 'I bought it at a festival,' she laughs. 'I took a train up but ended up driving it back!' She snags a booth at **E. Pellicci** (opposite left), **a Grade II listed greasy spoon on Bethnal Green Road with wood-panelled interiors. Serving full English breakfasts alongside Italian pastries** (opposite middle), **E. Pellicci opened in 1900 and has remained a family-run establishment ever since. A regular haunt of**

the Kray twins, E. Pellicci's **more recent visitors have included Jarvis Cocker, Ralph Fiennes and the entire cast of** *EastEnders*. **'We get builders, doctors, actors, directors,' says Anna Pellicci. 'Young people seem to all be directors nowadays. We must be the only people who make a cup of tea for a living!' Blonstein outside the establishment with Nevio Pellicci Jr** (opposite right), **whose father was born upstairs. 'They call me Queenie Queenie Bethnal Greenie here,' jokes Blonstein**

Talk to me about your relationship with derelict East End buildings.
I am the creative director and owner of a production agency for fashion and lifestyle events, and one of the main things we do is runways for fashion. We produce all the shows for London Fashion Week in the British Fashion Council hub. Derelict buildings are my absolute favourite, either building something where there is nothing or doing a show in a derelict building.

It would appear that many have moved to the East End to make something out of nothing. Is creation out of chaos particular to this part of the world?
It happens in any city. New York had it in the East Village; Cuba is starting it in Havana, and parts of Barcelona have it. It's often where a city has died because industrialisation has moved away and then artists and creatives move in. It's worked really well here. What I find fascinating, though, is how we are such leaders in fashion. The fashion designers that have come out of London's East End are extraordinary and unique, above and beyond anywhere else.

What is it about the East End that inspires style?
We are more liberal than most cities and also very inclusive. We don't care where you come from, what nationality you are, what religion you have. Kim Jones for Louis Vuitton, Jonathan Saunders, Gareth Pugh, are all from East London. This area has had a strong gay community and that's been good. It's funny in a way because you have this big Muslim community at the same time as this large gay community living side by side. The result is a magical melting pot. During the riots, the Muslim community protected all the shops, no matter what religion the owners were. They stood in Bethnal Green like an army preventing anything bad from happening. That's how strong the sense of community is out here.

You live on the canal ...
Living next to water is healing. I've literally spent hours out there sitting and contemplating life. I've also had many conversations with that big tree, next to the canal. I've asked him loads of questions. We've had baby swans, foxes, ducks, geese ...

Any special memories?
We had a great party on the canal and a hot tub during the Olympics with my dad's 1960s Super 8 screen and a video projector. Everyone on the bridge was watching with us. The neighbours, who are strict Muslims, came and partied with us too!

Define the East for me.
I've never, ever felt unsafe here. I've left my keys in the door numerous times ... The East is not about money; the East is about creativity and enjoying yourself.

'The fashion designers that have come out of London's East End are extraordinary and unique, above and beyond anywhere else'

Children's murals decorate the brick wall surrounding Columbia Primary School. 'People in the pubs would tell you stories that would go back to the war,' says freelance curator Catherine Lampert of the school. 'They'd talk about how this was a market with fresh fruit and vegetables.' Today the buzzing multicultural school educates children ranging in age from three to eleven throughout the year

PHILIP COLBERT

Pop Artist, Designer & Founder of The Rodnik Band

How would you describe yourself?
I guess I'm a jack-of-all-trades trying to make a world where I use all the different mediums I can get my hands on.

How did your creative adventure begin?
I was studying philosophy at university, and when I graduated in Scotland I set up a company selling scarves. The great thing about fashion is that it is the most democratic art, in the sense that it travels, it communicates, and it's freed from the confines of the gallery space. So it's a powerful medium. I wanted to re-contextualise the representation of clothing. Very quickly I realised that clothing offered a platform for expression, so I started introducing my philosophy into the line's marketing, branding and product design.

Would you say that fashion offers a language of its own?
Yeah. I started translating it into other products beyond clothing – into pictures, into sculpture, into furniture and various other things.

A lot of people associate your designs with Pop art …
Yes, definitely. I am interested in the power of symbols, so I try and identify key, iconic symbolic imagery that fits within my world of parody. I'll take a symbol that I find interesting – let's say meat or a fried egg – and make patterns out of it, make it decorative. It's sort of fun, but at the same time the decorative aspect communicates the idea.

So you believe in the power of creativity to affect people's thinking …
I am all about communication and trying to bring parody into everyday life. Obviously there have been designers in the past who have tried to push fashion on an intellectual level, but I attempt to platform it on a Pop level and on a basic, humorous and accessible level. I'm interested in bringing a sort of spirit out into the world, injecting fantasy, Pop and surrealism.

Philip Colbert phones a friend (opposite) **from his** *Pencil Chair* **(2015) amid his Pop-inspired designs outside the Yellow Submarine gallery on Columbia Road. 'I am definitely all about communication,' he says, 'about bringing parody into everyday life.' Using colourful symbols derived from consumer culture, he likes to surprise and amuse with imagery inspired by** **Americana, retro vehicles** (above) **or meat, lobsters and fried eggs (nods to Soutine and Francis Bacon). Colbert's multidisciplinary 'World of Art' also includes Pop clothing from his line The Rodnik Band. 'The great thing about fashion is that it's the most democratic art in the sense that it travels and it communicates, freed from the confines of a gallery space,' he observes**

You spent a lot of time in Notting Hill but decided to divorce yourself from that part of London and set up your home, your studio and your life in East London. Why?
I was drawn to East London because I used to go to New York regularly, and I fell in love with the buzz of the Lower East Side. The more I went to East London, the more I would identify similarities with downtown New York. I would get a sense that it was an area that was reinventing itself, an area with a strong historical and traditional element to it. I moved here four years ago. What I particularly like is that the whole city of London originated here. The Tower of London, the city walls … this is in a way the heart of real London. Obviously a lot was bombed and demolished, but there are pockets of brilliance and amazing layers of history. Quirky streets, pubs that have been here since the 1600s, old engravers … I like the 'Ye Olde' descriptions. It's all here!

What about the people?
I like the spirit of the people. I find it to be much more multicultural, and that is refreshing. The West is very comfortable, but creatively speaking it is quite flat. I identify more with the complete mix and chaos of East London.

You've just spent some time in LA. Is this something you foresee continuing to do in the future?
Yeah. I liked LA. I felt like a paintbrush that had been jammed into a DIY John Constable paint set, and then finally I was taken out and stuck into a Pop palette. Aesthetically speaking, LA offered the backdrop of what I am entirely about. There is a rich diversity of consumer Pop culture over there; the signage and details are all exaggerated and somehow free. I felt ideas could be bigger, with more gravity. Pop can live and dream in LA, and I'm at a point in my life where I really want to push ideas further. So it was nice to have fresh space to reinvent it all.

But it always feels good coming back to London, right?
Of course. Look at these butchers' and shops … They've all retained their original decorative aesthetic. You feel immediately tapped into lives that have been lived. It's the wallpaper of life. Take Bethnal Green, for example. It's authentic and it *gives* life. Hanging out on Bethnal Green Road is like art in the making!

'You feel immediately tapped into lives that have been lived. It's the wallpaper of life'

'Meat is a symbol of our mortality,' says Colbert, playfully demonstrating his case at his local butcher shop with artist Joe Sweeney and Emily Bryson (wearing The Rodnik Band's *Meat Sequin Dress*) (left). Calling Bethnal Green Road the 'Sunset Boulevard of East London', Colbert regularly explores his neighbourhood *en famille*, employing the shark pushchair he designed (below). His Franco-British wife Charlotte Colbert, a fellow artist and film-maker, enjoys the company of emoji masks (opposite) she created for her 2016 *Ordinary Madness* exhibition at Gazelli Art House. 'The emoticon is redefining our language,' she notes

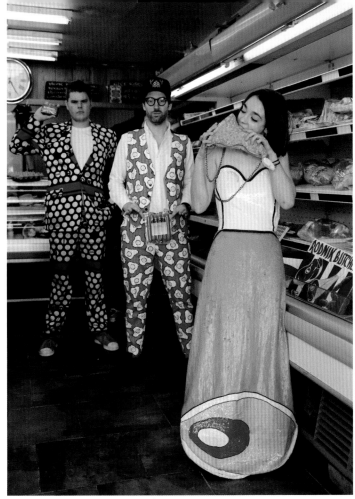

COLUMBIA ROAD FLOWER MARKET

'Columbia Road is the most charming street in the East End. On Sunday it becomes a vibrant jungle, and during the week it has a sleepy Victorian village vibe with the brilliant juxtaposition of city skyscrapers rising in the background'

Philip Colbert

A flower mart open on Sundays from 8.00 a.m. until 3.00 p.m. and featuring merchants who start setting up at 4.00 a.m., Columbia Road Flower Market includes stalls overflowing with flowers, trees and handmade crafts. Established in 1869 as a Saturday food market, Columbia Road evolved over time due to immigration pressures. An Act of Parliament moved it to Sundays to accommodate Jewish traders while the influx of Huguenots led to a demand for cut flowers and the fascination for caged songbirds. (A local pub called The Birdcage was founded in 1760.) After the Saturday market lapsed, the flower market continued to evolve, initially servicing the local population, many of whom had small gardens. Plants were brought in by handcart from market gardens in Hackney and Islington, and pitches were claimed on the day at the blow of a whistle. The area went into a decline in the 1970s but was saved from demolition by local pressure. Today Columbia Road Flower Market is internationally famous

CATHERINE LAMPERT

Art Historian & Curator

When did your love affair with the East End begin?
I graduated from college in the US and came back to London with my boyfriend. We heard we could get a live-in studio at Ravenscroft Studios, so we lived on Columbia Road from 1971 to 1976 and then bought a house just off Queensbridge Road, where I've lived ever since.

What was the mood like back then?
There were places that don't exist anymore, like a laundromat and a seafood shop, but The Birdcage is still here. It was a Jewish area, and people in the pub would tell stories about losing loved ones when a bomb dropped on the entrance to Bethnal Green Underground station. The pub would have live music. If one of the regulars died, they'd put their chair outside so when the funeral cart passed, it would come by their empty chair. They were very generous but a bit perplexed by the arrival of artists.

Was there a clash when the artists arrived?
In the early '70s, the artists were taking unoccupied buildings, so people could see them working hard and paying their rent. We weren't always able to gain trust, so we'd have to pay business rates, but eventually studio providers like SPACE or Acme took over leases. We would visit each other's studios. John Carter and Martin Palmer lived in Old Street. Hubert Dalwood had soirées in his Bethnal Green studio, and this building housed Clive Hodgson, John Cobb and Darcy Lange. We had a cellar below for people who wanted to do woodwork.

You've never left this part of London despite the changes.
There's a lot of continuity in between the changes. The fact that there's Council housing means the area will always have that mixture. On Queensbridge Road, though I'm now surrounded by bankers and lawyers, my next-door neighbours are still a family from Ghana, and at our street party every year, the person-of-honour is Mrs Brown, who's 104 years old and Jamaican.

Catherine Lampert on Columbia Road (opposite), **an area she has known intimately for the past forty years. Brawn, an East End restaurant** (left), **is located in a building that housed her studio/home in the early '70s. 'It was marvellous,' she says of the space**

Was there tension between following an artistic vocation and a community that may not have been open to the arts?
People have respect for individuals who live around here. It's not so much that they believe in the general policies of one community, or in regeneration, or in broadening horizons, because those people would say, 'My horizons are already broad.' Artists would say, 'We don't feel élite because our children attend the same schools.' Dialogue and respect always work.

Over time, will the area retain a visionary outlook, its sense of identity and its central role in promoting creativity?
I have worries. There are parts of Tower Hamlets, like every single Council, that are under pressure to keep their social services going. As long as they don't re-zone this area to high-rises and spread Aldgate's scene north, then it's going to be terrific. There's always going to be extreme mixtures.

Since 1978 you've spent every Friday up in Mornington Crescent, another 'home' of sorts.
Every Friday for a few hours, I visit Frank [Auerbach], who has been in the same studio since 1954, taking it over from Leon Kossoff, who was born close to where we are now. There's only five of us that Frank sees on a regular basis apart from the newsagent and hairdressers that are local to him, so we bring him the world.

Has Frank Auerbach managed to capture your soul, do you think?
It's always going to be his soul as well as mine. If there's a hint of a previous painting, he won't accept it. It's harder and harder for me, but I always come out elated. He knows the sitters so well that he will detect if you're preoccupied by something, distracted, tired, under a lot of stress, or equally if something is going well in your life. He picks up what he likes from decades and decades of experience.

Going back to the East, tell me a bit about Leon Kossoff.
Leon Kossoff was born on Sydney Road, but his family was living in Arnold Circus when he was young. About six years ago he returned to Arnold Circus to draw the bandstand and various buildings – a form of coming home. The buildings there are one of the first purpose-built estates. To Leon, it meant a lot to reconnect with the area through drawing. And he used Leila's as a resting place for tea!

Lampert inspects fresh fruit and veg on display (above) at Leila's Shop, which she's been patronising for a long time. In fact, she held her wedding party in the café next door. Leila's has also been popular with local artists (right). Lampert surveys Brawn's open kitchen (opposite). Though she has witnessed dramatic changes to the area, she sees them as minor in comparison to those witnessed by East Enders before her time. 'People in the pub would tell you stories that would go back to the war ... about people they lost when a bomb dropped on the entrance to Bethnal Green Underground station, or about how Columbia Primary School was a market with fresh fruit and vegetables. They saw losses that you couldn't match now,' she explains. 'In this territory, I've lived my whole adult life ... The stones, the brick, the architecture, it's so familiar. I know it like the back of my hand'

'Dialogue and respect always worked with the community'

The iconic Oval Gasometer, now tethered to Oval Space, an arts and event space in Bethnal Green, towers above Hackney and can be seen from Cambridge Heath to Broadway Market. Featuring sixteen classical-style columns, it was used to store gas in Victorian times. Built by John Clark in 1866 with Westwood and Wrights of Dudley, the Oval Gasometer and others like it have been saved from destruction by the East End Waterway Group, among others. Since 2012, Network Rail have been selling or redeveloping them into housing or workspaces

CONOR DONLON

Founder of Donlon Books

Conor Donlon (opposite) **in his shop, Donlon Books, which he founded in 2006. Offering a selection of rare volumes for sale, Donlon focuses on photography, art, fashion and critical theory, as well as LGBTQ, erotica and counterculture literature** (above)**. Supporting independent publishers and even publishing himself, he also hosts launches and screenings for the likes of Wolfgang Tillmans, David Armstrong and Viviane Sassen** (left)

'Conor's bookshop is a beautifully curated wonderland that seamlessly merges fashion, art and lifestyle. It is a place that sustains the imagination'

Lyall Hakaraia

BROADWAY MARKET

Broadway Market has been in existence since the 1890s, and today sells a variety of fresh food, street food and products created by local designers, as well as featuring artists' stalls

AMELIA TROUBRIDGE

Portrait, Commercial & Documentary Photographer

Would you agree that North Londoners are consumers while East Londoners are creators?
Yes. That's why I've stayed here. Most of my family and friends are in West London, but I found I couldn't focus on what I wanted to achieve personally or creatively being in that environment. I grew up in South London and wanted to travel the world. I was nineteen when I was introduced to this guy who had just bought a brewery in East London and told me to come see it. So off I go to Brick Lane. Though I'd grown up in London, I had never been there in my life. I didn't even know East London existed! Lo and behold, I found the Truman Brewery, and within six months we'd done up this beautiful space which was derelict with pigeons. We called it The Brickhouse and lived and worked there. I lived in a room which had a 15-metre-high ceiling and was one of the first four occupants of the Truman Brewery.

What years are we talking about?
Mid-'90s. I started a not-for-profit gallery where we had photo shoots to pay the rent. I was also part of that amazing club scene like Ministry of Sound. We had these great parties that I did with Nick Love, who is now a famous club owner in West London. Nick Love's first parties at the Truman Brewery were absolutely

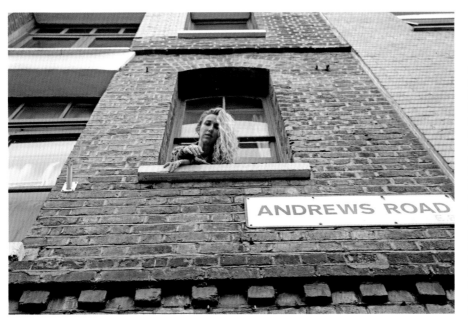

Amelia Troubridge looks down on Andrews Road in Hackney (left) from the Georgian terraced house she bought in 2005. A self-taught photographer, Troubridge was one of the early tenants at Truman Brewery in the mid-1990s. Her rooftop (opposite) overlooks the area of London which she has called home since she was young. 'Why did I come to East London? What was in East London that wasn't anywhere else?' she wonders out loud. 'It was space. Space to create and to be, without boundaries'

outrageous. At that time I was doing reportage photojournalism. *Esquire* would send me to America, *Days of the World* was sending me to Colombia, so I was living this extraordinary life. Then I bought in Shoreditch in 2000. You know why I came to East London? It was space: space to create, to be, to identify with myself, without boundaries. That's why I stayed here. I thought I was going to leave London, but instead the world came to us in East London.

How would you define your tribe?
The one I was brought up in consisted of women who didn't go out and had no careers. They married young and were very good at cooking, raising children. They never tested boundaries or rebelled or questioned. I've always questioned. I've always tried to evolve, and I never went for the easy option.

How do you feel about East London now?
What is very sad is seeing this part of London being eroded in the last decade. People who have a big heart and a lot of love to give but aren't motivated by money are finding it harder and harder to survive. What I love about East London is the amazing network of people who love helping each other out. People will go, 'What's my skill and what's your skill? Let's help each other.'

Troubridge encounters her friend Sara Blonstein on a rainy Andrews Road (left). As someone who has straddled the boundary between glossy fashion portraits and gritty documentaries, Troubridge has shot the likes of David Cameron and Dita Von Teese. 'Photography, especially my area of photography, has struggled to keep identification and value in the digital area,' she acknowledges. Enjoying a smoke with the now obsolete Bethnal Green gas holder behind her (above), she ponders Victorian at-risk constructions: 'What is sad is seeing this part of London being corroded'

'It was space. Space to create
and to be, without boundaries'

An art installation by Mobster on Pedley Street tests viewers' engagement with public space by means of subversive comments

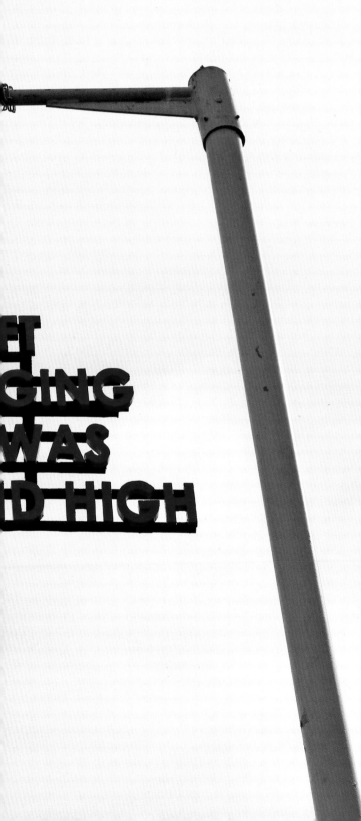

VIKTOR WYND

As well as being a pataphysicist, you're an artist, are you not?
It's irrelevant. If what I do and think is *art*, then yes, but it doesn't matter if it's art. It's just a name.

Didn't you study art history?
I studied Islamic history at SOAS. I had a scholarship to go to Isfahan University and they wouldn't give me a visa. I was pretty miffed so I did a foundation and postgrad instead. I'm interested in narrative structures. I write as well. I'm particularly interested in people who are multidisciplinary.

Why did you set up shop in East London?
Because it's cheap. It's not cheap now, but it was cheap when I came here. I wanted a lot of space and I didn't have money to pay for it.

Would you say that there is a stronger imaginative spirit here vs the rest of the city?
Rich people en masse tend to be very dull. It's the ghetto that's creative.

How would you describe Mare Street?
Mareditch is Shoreditch in estate agents' slang. Mare Street I always liked as it was traditionally the dump at the end of the world, full of crap corner shops and launderettes that didn't work. This place is now flooded with smart restaurants. It's still 90 per cent shit, but it's changing. If I was fifteen years younger, I wouldn't look to London and Hackney any more.

Where would you be looking instead?
Probably Margate or Hastings. If Hackney was the same as it was nine years ago, we'd be living round the corner from here, but we can't afford it any more. My place now is ten minutes from the beach; it's a Tudor house. There are fields, woodlands, barns, and it costs the same as a one-bed flat around here.

Viktor Wynd outside his museum of curiosities, **The Last Tuesday Society** (opposite) **on Mare Street. 'It's supposed to be the inside of my head,'** he explains of his lair of eccentricity. His pale pink Vespa alerts visitors to his being at home; on offer is an extraordinary display of tea, a guidebook and access to an extraordinary display of artefacts, ranging from taxidermy lions and collections of crustaceans (left) **to shrunken heads** obtained by Wynd on his travels. **'Some things sparkle and some things don't,'** he says by way of explaining his collecting habits. **'If something interests me, I grasp it'**

Where do you find your inspiration these days?
I'm much more interested in nature. There's plenty of nature and less drink.

Tell me about the Last Tuesday Society.
It's supposed to be the inside of my head. I just want people to come inside and share the space, as it can be quite a lonely little place.

And what about the contents of your little den of curiosities?
Well, some things sparkle and some things don't. I'm a magpie so I don't concentrate on one thing for very long. If something interests me, I grab it.

Did the story start in your childhood?
It's not so much *when* it started, because every child collects toy cars and shells he/she finds on the beach but then grows out of it. It just never stopped for me. This place was originally designed as an art project. I wanted to build a Dadaist anti-institution shop with an interesting script.

But why a 'museum'?
I like old museums and higgledy-piggledy things. In some ways, this place lives in the tradition of pre-Enlightenment museums. I couldn't find a proper curiosity shop in England so I opened this! There is the Pataphysical Museum in Highgate which is still amazing.

Why are you attracted by the bizarre, the occult, the different and the uniquely dark?
Well, André Breton wanted to see what was on the other side of boredom; for me, eye candy's the trigger. Also, I can't afford an élite brooch, but I can afford a dead wasp which is just as beautiful. I can't afford a piece of twelfth-century gold that was made to hold a bezoar, but I can afford a bezoar.

How do you go about constantly finding this plethora of novelty items?
Perseverance and curiosity. If you look, you find, I assure you!

The skeleton of a lion (above) **surveys the basement of The Last Tuesday Society. The ground-floor cocktail bar offers a dizzying range of eclectic drinks based on the oddities in Wynd's collection. A former call centre, the space also acts as a gallery space for** exhibitions, lectures and parties. A self-proclaimed dandy, Wynd wanders down Hare Row in his fur coat (opposite). **'If Hackney was the same as it was nine years ago, we'd be living round the corner from here, but now we can't afford it,'** he laments. **'Time defines who we are and what we do'**

'Rich people en masse tend to be very dull. It's the ghetto that's creative'

AMECHI IHENACHO

Stylist & Tailor, Owner of The Pattern

French-Nigerian stylist and pattern cutter Amechi Ihenacho (opposite) outside his shop on Hackney Road, where he keeps unusual vintage clothing (left) collected as inspiration while working as a fashion editor. 'I'm quite good at finding things,' he explains. 'This shop is petite, but I love it because it means I can cram everything in and find ways of always changing it.' Cutting patterns for both women and men, Ihenacho enjoys a challenge, noting, 'I'm working on a triple-breasted coat at the moment'

'We are all just little towns in London, aren't we? This is quite an intense town with loads of different people. You've got your 1 to 10. The 1 could be the bum in the street and the 10 could be the person looking for a Chanel bag'

MATTHEW KILLICK

Artist

Matthew Killick has been in his Hackney studio (right and below) **for nearly five years, having previously squatted or used cheap studios 'surfing on a wave of development and destruction' which have since been condemned. 'I never thought I would squat,' Killick says. 'But I set up a show in a gallery space with a load of artists, and after the show had finished, no-one booted us out of the space because it was badly derelict. There were pigeons in there, rats, foxes ... It was the real thing. Broken windows ...**

I was sleeping on a door resting on two chairs for about two years; it was like living on what you could find on the street and making art. I try and not go to work so I can spend my time making paintings.' Killick works mostly in monochrome, using smooth surfaces like board and glass to create ultra-flat paintings. The work behind him (opposite) **is from a series of large backlit glass panels titled Postcards from the Deep, commissioned by the Great Eastern Wall Gallery, London's largest outdoor gallery space**

'I was surfing on a wave of development and destruction and getting those spaces cheaply because they were condemned'

LIVE EEL F.Co

HOT and JELLIED
EELS

OOKE IMPORTER

Established in 1900, F. Cooke is the last remaining eel, liquor, pie and mash shop in Broadway Market. This family-run establishment sticks to their traditions; they don't use knives and *never* sell gravy.

They have a regular cohort of customers, including pensioners who grew up in the area and come in for the £1 OAP special – a hearty meal of mash, pie and creamy parsley liquor

PABLO FLACK & DAVID WADDINGTON

Restaurateurs & Founders of Bistrotheque & Hoi Polloi

You've both been active on the East End hospitality scene since the dawn of time …

Pablo: We didn't invent the East End; there were older artist-types who were already embedded in the area. The Bricklayers Arms, where we started working together, cemented the social scene which grew into all those horrible bars in Shoreditch. To be fair, all roads lead back to the likes of Jonny Woo and Richard [Battye], who owned The George & Dragon.

David: The East End started to have a rebirth after an economic collapse where a lot of property in Shoreditch became vacant. People like estate agent James Goff marketed directly to creatives. It was the beginning of Brit Art and Cool Britannia so you ended up with a snowball effect of cultural movements that all crossed over.

Pablo: The Bricklayers Arms in the mid-'90s wasn't inhabited by the most successful artists at the time; maybe the best known was McQueen. They all have now become quite popular so they must have been working really hard to get their shit together.

David Waddington and Pablo Flack (opposite) opened Bistrotheque in Hackney in 2004. 'What we've always done,' explains Flack, 'is sell culture and a social experience along with food and drink.' The duo have worked together since the mid-1990s at The Bricklayers Arms – 'You can trace a lot of creative roads back to it,' notes Flack. Waddington and Flack on Vyner Street (left), a popular arts outpost

Was there a sort of creative chemical reaction?
Pablo: Shoreditch set a tone for people working together, freelancing, and networks of people feeding off of each other. That was fuelled by freedom of movement. I see Brexit as the death of that.

David: Everything we've done is because we have been able to move around and have had influences from across Europe and the world. Everyone would flock here from abroad, so it became internationally important. The East End has been everything for everybody.

Pablo: Shoreditch was fed in waves, first the Swedish, then the South Americans coming in with Spanish passports. That was a lot of the George & Dragon scene, a mix of Jonny Woo alt-drag with a bunch of crazy South Americans. Older, very English people don't understand the effect that had on the economy. The reason that the tech centre has grown is because of that exact culture, especially around the East End. I am pro-immigration as I've only seen the benefits, and I'm afraid London will be the most damaged by Brexit. People started to leave in 2010/11, and more and more of my Facebook group is now outside the UK.

You've been at the forefront of key cultural initiatives. What does this mean for the hospitality business?
Pablo: What we sell is culture and a social experience. Food and drink matter to us and so does service, but we're not saying, 'Oh there's a new mushroom that's just come out' because it's not going to make the party any better. (If it will, we'll make sure to throw it in the mix!) When we opened 333 Mother Bar in 1997, we did installations to entertain ourselves, and they were really effective marketing. We did parties where we turfed the inside of the club, we made it snow, all these crazy things. The parties were full of creative people. Today at Bistrotheque, we can have a giant cock ring by Prem Sahib up as a Christmas decoration, and we treat people to a good time. We could have gotten much bigger, but it doesn't interest us. It's got no soul. I'm fine working in other neighbourhoods as cities are fluid, but the fun lies in finding creative people.

Waddington and Flack at Bistrotheque (above)**, a converted 1930s clothing factory with painted concrete floors and brick walls, now hosting a bar, restaurant and performance space which has featured the inimitable Jonny Woo. Though the duo remain committed to their independent space, a partnership with Ace Hotel has resulted in Hoi Polloi** (opposite) **and a new space in the West End. 'We're like independent record labels,'** summarises Flack. **'We value independence'**

'*What we sell is culture and a social experience along with food and drink*'

Pablo Flack

NIMROD KAMER

Journalist & Writer

The always playful Nimrod Kamer (opposite) **enjoys breakfast at home in Tower Hamlets with Natasha Arselan, founder of AucArt, an online auction platform dedicated to artworks by graduates. Behind the colourful couple hangs a recent purchase by Kristaps Ancans. 'I used to only go to art events to meet** people and I didn't care about the art,' says Kamer. 'Now I go to see the art and I don't care about the people.' Kamer continues his breakfast outdoors at Allpress Espresso Bar (above). 'It's not a hotspot, it's a cold spot,' he deadpans. 'It's a Dalston uncooked breakfast of champions'

What do you like about Hackney?
It's a great way to see the stars. When you're in town, there is lots of light pollution, but there is less light in Hackney. I use an app called SkyView to see the planets.

It's true that you get better views as the buildings are lower in the East. It was bombed during the Second World War, wasn't it?
There are still bombs in the canal. They'll explode one day and people will use it as a social media event.

Did you come straight to Hackney from Israel in 2010?
Yes. I did some stuff for Israeli TV, and when I moved here I started pitching to newspapers and kept pushing local stories in Hackney. The first story I did was 'How to Sneak into Members' Clubs' in the *Evening Standard*. It's hard to annoy anyone in Hackney by doing investigative journalism. People don't have much to hide.

Is what you see what you get, then?
Exactly. What you see in the West is the opposite of what you get. I also kept pitching people to do their Wikipedia page because I am obsessed with Wikipedia.

Why? Because you can control the content?
I love the language; it makes me feel like I can programme. Also, you don't know what someone does, so you write a Wikipedia page to get to know them.

What's your main interest?
Class and class warfare. I'm obsessed with Trump, Bernie Sanders, Corbyn and politics. Living in Hackney, all of my friends are broke. My friends and I realised that living in London has made us conservative. The chase for property and invoices makes you become a Tory in a way. Everyone I know who does self-assessment wants to avoid paying taxes because they feel they spend too much money and have no money for taxes. I had a few suits made recently by this local tailor, and I find it hard go to London Fields with a proper tailor-made suit, so I put a coat on until I get to the West. You cannot show people you have stuff when you live in Hackney.

You once told me about a specific Hackney language that is largely social-media-based. Would you say that it correlates with the area's demographic?
Yeah. Many people want to use emojis, and there's 'emojinal' and 'emojinal blackmail'. There's also 'promasturbate', which is 'procrastinate' and 'masturbate'. People use 'YOLO' a lot, as in 'you only live once'; 'YOLO fever' is the new yellow fever. You also have 'gorgeois' if you're both 'gorgeous' and 'bourgeois'.

Tell me more about Hackney's particular brand of reverse psychology.
Many people are rich here. Their parents are from Surrey, but they always pretend to be poor, even if they're not. (Which is not fair for the not-so-wealthy people.) They 'downgrade' themselves all the time. There was Occupy St Paul's, but how can you afford to go sit for two weeks and not work? It's all about trust funds basically. I'm writing a sitcom called *Hard Left*, which is a big joke on left-wing people who pretend to be poor. I also did *#DIGIDATING*, which is an online blind-date show for ASO. It was one girl, three guys, and all the questions she asked them were social media questions. There was a glory hole through which they'd feel each other's phone to see if it was a Samsung or a BlackBerry. There's also the comedy about finding love on UberPool, and I'm doing a social-climbing guide in the East.

How would you like to be remembered?
As a social climber.

Kamer visits the Costume Studio on Balls Pond Road with his gun-wielding friend (and model) Django Chan-Reeves (above). **Having found the perfect outfit, Kamer waits patiently at Dalston Kingsland Overground station** (right), **styling himself 'the king of Kingsland Overground'. The station is a dividing line for access to UberPool, a fact on which Kamer has capitalised in his latest comedy. Having donned Happy Socks and a modified Trump campaign cap** (opposite), **he samples Korean fare at Hurwundeki, the Korean café and hair salon near Cambridge Heath station. His sights set on being 'a Hackney MP one day', he jokingly reads** *Trump: The Art of the Deal* **for inspiration**

'Many here use UberPool. They get to know new people ... it's the new dating app in a way'

Hurwundeki, which combines a hair salon and a Korean restaurant with an antiques and clothing boutique, was established by Ki-Chul Lee in 2004 as an all-encompassing lifestyle brand next to Cambridge Heath station. The shabby-chic interior with its industrial vibe and mismatched decor embodies one of the East End's pioneering aesthetics. A top Seoul hairdresser before coming to London to study with Vidal Sassoon, Ki-Chul set up shop in East London after forays into clothing retail and coffee shops. Early on, his customers included Kate Moss and Pete Doherty. Hurwundeki, his current hideaway (one of three in London), has become a popular stop for £9 haircuts, freshly prepared Korean barbecue and coffee

MAUREEN PALEY

Founder & Director of Maureen Paley

Tell me how a young American woman in the '70s decided to root her career in the East End of London.
I came to London in '77. I had read in the *International Herald Tribune* about Vivienne Westwood and Jordan [Mooney], so I wanted to see how it was unfolding. I had studied at Brown University and was aware of Gilbert & George on Fournier Street. I wanted to look at where the artists lived. The dusty streets near Spitalfields Market fascinated me. I remember walking through the partly functioning/partly derelict market to get to Fournier Street to see their house and compare it to the place I had seen from afar as a student. The desire to be in the area grew from my exploration. I was also looking for loft spaces like I had known from New York's Lower East Side and SoHo. Acme Housing Association had housing for artists in the East End, and I had just applied to the Royal College of Art. I remember saying, 'If I get my MA acceptance and if I get a place to live in London, I'll stay on.' Both things came through. I came to Beck Road and developed the site as a studio space and place to live. That grew into me staying there but also was my first iteration as a gallery. In April 1984 I created Interim Art. In '83 I had gone to New York and looked at Pat Hearn, Colin de Land, Jay Gorney, Nature Morte and International With Monument – spaces run by young people doing experimental work. That gave me strength to bring some energy back to London. The first ten years of the gallery in that space were very experimental; it was a labour of love. When people talk about the gentrification of the East End, we were doing urban renewal. We were engaged in a complete re-examining of places that had been seen as derelict.

Do good ideas stem from dereliction?
They do. The creative community is often open to premises that others might abandon or feel have no potential. Because we were able to create out of nothing, often that abandonment and neglect would give us a measure of possibility. The East End is testimony to that. The '70s to the '90s were a key moment.

Maureen Paley walks through the Witan Street underpass (left) and passes the local auto repair shop (opposite) en route to her namesake gallery on Herald Street. Paley has taken on the risk of renewing many derelict East London spots, having lived in East London since the late 1970s as part of the artistic community. 'We were able to create something from nothing, and that abandonment and neglect give you a measure of possibility,' she remembers

Paley prepares for an exhibition entitled *Stages* with American artist Tom Burr (above). **They review Burr's *Sexual Soft Target*, a mixed-media piece partly composed of military blankets, exploring the memories and emotions that objects retain. 'I think the international spirit is what drove my gallery from the early days,' explains Paley. 'I wouldn't take personal credit necessarily, but I'm definitely part of something that helped the growth of creativity in the area'**

Is the East End still as exciting today?

In thirty or forty years you would expect that things would change. There are dangers with change because things can be lost in the mix, extinguished or somehow pressurised. That's never good. But change does occur, and it's not like it happened overnight. People like to say it did, but I remember when I first moved to the area, many people were not supportive and did not feel comfortable.

You're one of the few artistic personalities who has stuck to her guns by staying here. A lot of galleries eventually moved west.

I had a quick foray into the West End, but my wings were singed very badly so I came back here with renewed love and no further desire to leave. Staying in the East End meant I watched things happen in the area like Gillian Wearing and Wolfgang Tillmans get the Turner Prize. The south-east grew when Tate Modern opened. So there was a lot of activity that gave waves of energy to what we were doing. The international spirit is what drove my gallery from the early days. I was bringing a lot from abroad alongside showcasing people from the whole of Great Britain. My commitment to the area is super-real. Places that are under-considered to me are super-exciting. It's to do with one's sense of adventure. Gilbert & George have that sense of adventure, that pioneering spirit. If that's your spirit, you can feel frustrated when everything's too nice, too polished, too corporate. When I first came here, a lot was missing so I would often be pushed to find those items in the rest of the city. That meant investigative work. Today I can go to Broadway Market and get a book at Conor Donlon's bookshop or go to Artwords or to the Broadway Bookshop. I can have whole days when I don't need to leave the East anymore.

Have you personally had a regenerative influence on the area?

The whole of the arts have. I wouldn't take personal credit; I'm part of something. Chisenhale Gallery, the Whitechapel and Raven Row have engaged a lot of artists. Artists such as Gillian Wearing, Michael Landy and Rebecca Warren have their studios here. From the beginning, the area was rich with activity, energy and thinking. People believed in it, and there was a lot of mutual support. Being the first person on the street, it's so exciting to now have Herald St, Campoli Presti, THE RYDER, Laura Bartlett and Breese Little nearby. White Cube were here for a while. I was always close to The Approach as well as Carl Freedman. These galleries and many more make a contribution. In the early days, I was aware of being an outpost and a destination; however, with time we all were very collegiate and the area has grown around us.

Having started exhibiting out of her East End home in 1984, Paley moved to her current premises on Herald Street (bottom) in 1999, and has been credited with nurturing a number of art superstars such as Rebecca Warren, Gillian Wearing and Wolfgang Tillmans, whose studio was once at nearby Morain House (below) on Cambridge Heath Road: 'I watched Wolfgang Tillmans and Gillian Wearing grow and get the Turner Prize … I saw things happen in the area and people opened up.' Though the street was once empty (right), Herald Street is now home to a number of successful galleries

'We were engaged in a complete re-examining of places that had been seen as derelict'

McQUEENS

Located in an arch on Cambridge Heath Road, McQueens florists have a presentation room at the front and a floristry school upstairs. Intending to offer the highest-quality, best-presented seasonal flower 'installations', Kally Ellis rescued the failing shop in Shoreditch in 1991 and named it after Alexander McQueen's aunt, who had run it before her. With no formal floristry training, Ellis built the business through word of mouth.

McQueens' style focuses on simplicity and skill, selecting vases and props for maximum impact. McQueens stocks clients such as Mulberry, the Oscars ceremony in Hollywood and the White House annual Correspondents' Association Dinner, and boasts an offshoot shop at Claridge's. Here a hydrangea bouquet is readied for afternoon tea at the Berkeley Hotel in Knightsbridge, with pale green carnations heading out to a wedding in Mayfair

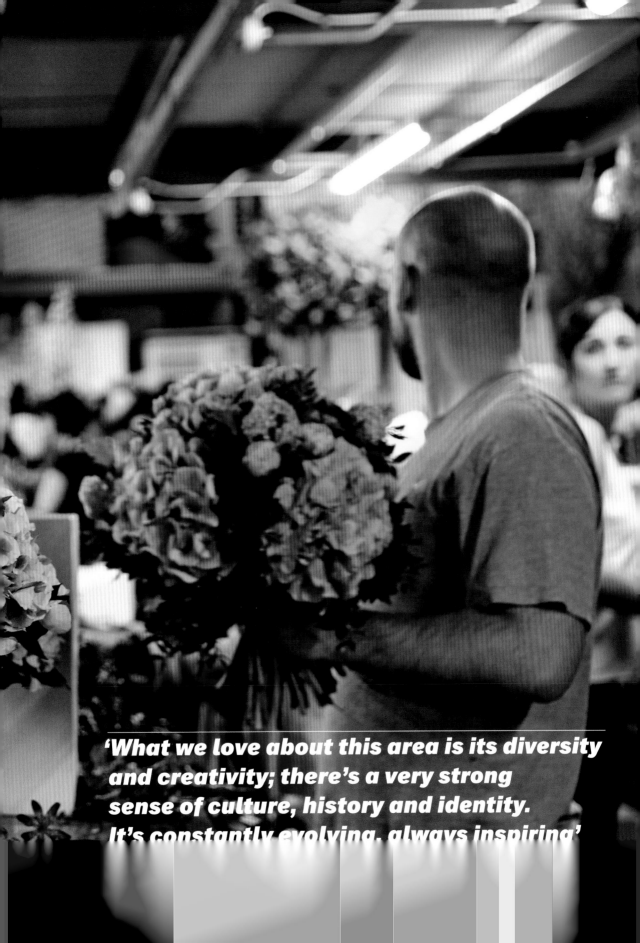

'What we love about this area is its diversity and creativity; there's a very strong sense of culture, history and identity. It's constantly evolving, always inspiring'

NIKKI

Cabbie

East End taxi driver Nikki has his MOT done by Chris, owner of Coborn Garage on Three Colts Lane (above). Tucked away behind Bethnal Green, Three Colts Lane remains a locus for mechanics, metalwork and cab centres yet is just moments away from the concentration of contemporary art galleries on Herald Street (opposite). 'You don't get the warm feel anymore here,' Nikki observes with regret. 'We were people who said hello and loved a good chat. You don't even know who's living next to you any more.'

A paperboy for the area's elderly women when he was a child, Nikki's memories feel disconnected from current redevelopment trends. 'I once nicked a chimpanzee and took him home,' he says when passing Dressage Court, an animal home in the 1950s. Born in Ireland, Nikki knew the Kray brothers. 'If the Kray brothers were still alive,' he notes, 'this lot wouldn't be walking around with knives, believe me,' he observes of today's petty criminals. 'We would still have safe streets to ourselves'

'Do you know what the difference between Ronnie and Reggie and the Norwich Union was? Ronnie and Reggie actually stopped people from getting burgled!'

BARNABY CARDER

Spoon Carver & Owner of the Shop Barn the Spoon

'One of the things that I find quite boring in this country is that I'm always portrayed as a humble craftsman. It's very linked to our class system, because it's not like that in Japan and it's not like that in Scandinavia'

Barnaby Carder got into woodwork when he was twelve and lived in the woods for a time, with only a 'tarp between two trees' to call home. He started making spoons to get by. Deeming himself a 'sell-out', he now owns a popular shop. Carder gravitated to Hackney Road due to the strong local tradition of woodworking. He co-founded Spoonfest, an international summer gathering of carvers

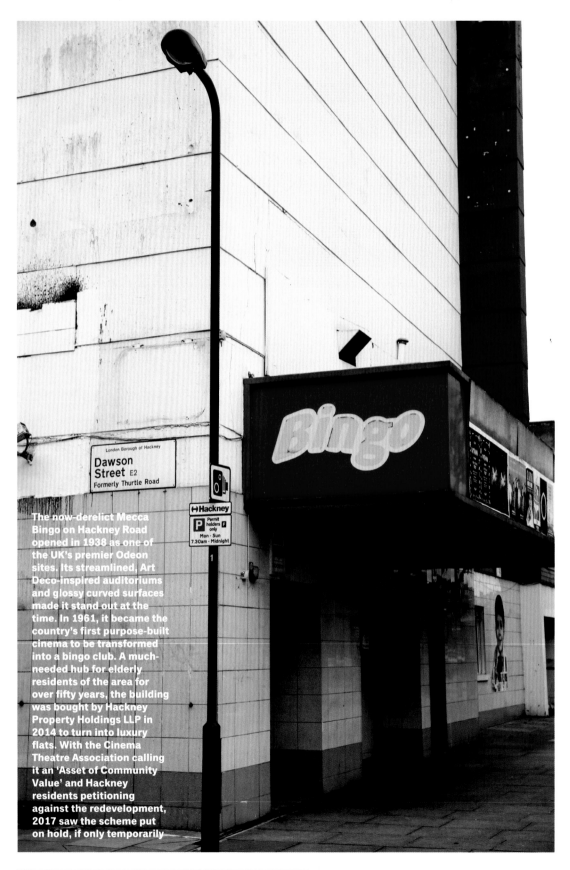

The now-derelict Mecca Bingo on Hackney Road opened in 1938 as one of the UK's premier Odeon sites. Its streamlined, Art Deco-inspired auditoriums and glossy curved surfaces made it stand out at the time. In 1961, it became the country's first purpose-built cinema to be transformed into a bingo club. A much-needed hub for elderly residents of the area for over fifty years, the building was bought by Hackney Property Holdings LLP in 2014 to turn into luxury flats. With the Cinema Theatre Association calling it an 'Asset of Community Value' and Hackney residents petitioning against the redevelopment, 2017 saw the scheme put on hold, if only temporarily

GEORGE LAMB
& COLM ROCHE

Founders & Hosts of Radio Wolfgang

How did the two of you connect?
George: It was an ideological connection. Colm ran a branding agency, I worked in entertainment, and we met through a show I was doing on the BBC. We realised we both felt slightly frustrated with the way the world was going and with our related input. He'd just won a contract with Unilever and was doing a Lynx campaign where he found himself enlarging the already perfectly sized breasts of this model …
Colm: Well, they requested it, but I refused and they left. I was thinking, Is this my contribution to the world?'
George: Yeah. I woke up one day and I was a game-show host and wasn't entirely sure how that happened. I thought, This is your legacy. You're going to be complicit in selling distraction to poor people.

So you set up Wolfgang?
Colm: Yes. We wanted something that would transcend age, race and class. The media ghettoises, so you'll have a middle-class English family reading the *Telegraph* and listening to Radio 4 next door to a West Indian family listening to Choice FM. Although they live next door, they don't know anything about each other's cultures. If I say 'Wolfgang' to my white middle-class mum in the countryside, she thinks of Mozart and feels safe. If I say 'Wolfgang' to a street kid from Peckham, it's a pseudonym for Odd Future – a rap group – and he wants to check it out.

So, from gameshow hosting and branding, you've become opinion makers. That's a big responsibility.
Colm: We wanted this to be inclusive rather than exclusive. We wanted to be a community rather than a single editorial maxim. Our problem with media is that it all comes from one person's opinion – an editor, a journalist, a photographer. We live in an age of collaboration, community and self-generated content, so we wanted to integrate that into the media. We've now got an audience that doesn't trust the media and who are also overexposed to information. They are passive and disillusioned and have disclosure fatigue from the level of information coming in. We wanted to create a platform controlled by its audience.

Colm Roche and George Lamb at Radio Wolfgang (opposite). **Listeners determine content, which varies from music to documentaries to talk radio. 'We live in an age where it's all about collaboration, community and self-generated content,' explains Roche, 'so we wanted to try and integrate that into the media.' Lamb and Roche beneath the railway arch** (below) **of Martello Terrace en route to their favourite local bakery, E5 Bakehouse**

Lamb and Roche wait to order at E5 (opposite), an organic bakery in a London Fields railway arch with an onsite stone mill. 'Ben [Mackinnon] is the number-one sourdough guy in London,' says Lamb, 'but he's not greedy. He only produces a finite amount, otherwise he'll just become Tesco's.' The duo head to London Fields (left), where they regularly walk and discuss ideas. 'A lot of Wolfgang has been figured out pacing round London Fields,' laughs Lamb. Drovers used the Hackney park for grazing before taking livestock to slaughter

Did you have a particular focus for this platform?
Colm: Information is consumed increasingly in bite-sized segments. People aren't reading long articles any more; we believe that audio is the new long-form article. With Wolfgang, you've got long-form, in-depth discussions or documentaries that you can listen to on the train, when you're running or while you're in the garden.

Why set up in the East End?
George: We moved here because there are a bunch of like-minded people around, and because we're in an area where you can rent a nice big space and you don't have to pay through the nose. You've got a lot of opinion leaders round here and a lot of early adopters. I've been living round here for seven or eight years. I'm from West London and he's from Cork. It was a weird thing to come east as when I grew up, the East was just rough …

Where did you grow up?
George: Fulham. My dad's gran was born in Whitechapel, and everyone from my dad's side is from Whitechapel/ Bethnal Green. He said, 'You don't want to go round there! It's a shithole.' I remember coming in 1990 and it was wild, like a war zone. It's funny that years later you

find yourself migrating back. I don't know if it's in my DNA or what. The more time I spent here the more I realised that all the interesting young people who were thinking outside the box were here. The frequency is totally different here. Not just positivity but possibility. People give things a go and people support it.
Colm: There's also a spirit of independence. People shy away from the bigger brands.

What about any challenges or concerns for the future?
George: There's a cycle that happens. Property is cheap, artists move in and make it cool, rich folks want a piece of that, then it's not cool anymore, and it pushes the artists out. Maybe we'll all live in Norfolk in these amazing artist communities! There are huge droves of people moving to Margate. There's been a brain drain in the metropolis.

What sort of mark would you like to leave?
George: It's about getting a discourse going. Our remit is to be positive and solution-based. We're going to focus on what's right in the world and see how we can create a truly interwoven ecosystem of humanity, classes and creativity. That is what we care about.

'We moved here because there are a bunch of like-minded people around ... You've got a lot of opinion leaders round here and a lot of early adopters'

George Lamb

As part of East London's regeneration, rooftops are becoming an increasingly popular hang-out for locals. London Fields Roof Gardens (pictured) is located on top of FieldWorks, a design, arts and social enterprise community. The rooftop, which hosts music and art events over the summer months, overlooks London Fields and the nearby Overground, giving a rare viewpoint of the transport system that connects East London to the rest of the city. With Mayor Sadiq Khan set to introduce a 24-hour service on the weekends from December 2017, connecting Hackney to Lewisham, accessibility to the area's cultural life to include galleries, eateries and nightlife will no doubt be increased

COLIN ROTHBART

**Founder of The Shed Parties, TV Producer
& Co-founder of The Glory**

Colin Rothbart outside The Shed (opposite)**, a private party venue where East End creatives mix with celebrity DJs and off-duty drag performers for evenings of pure hedonism. 'I received an ASBO letter from a neighbour which said, "It's alleged that you have frequent gatherings at your house with nudity,"' laughs Rothbart, 'but we don't have parties as much now.' Built as an inexpensive extension to his London Fields house, The Shed's colourful exterior (by Alex Noble) is just one of many vivid details. Reclining on red satin sheets 'taken from a hotel in Dubai' and sporting a jacket made in Cape Town, Rothbart reflects on his newly installed mirrored ceiling** (above) – **'a nightmare!'**

Tell me about this fun house of yours!
It's a shared house. I come from a family of four in North London, I lived in Soho for six years by myself, but I missed living with lots of people. I made the house quite bespoke and I've just put weird mirror ceilings all over it. It was a nightmare. I don't want to spend any more money on the house, but I always say that and then something else comes along.

Is the house a self-portrait?
It must be. My friend Phil describes it as the aftermath of a tsunami! When I first moved in, it was just like the place next door. I got it really cheap because I didn't realise this was a crime hotspot. When I first moved here, there were lots of guys sitting on my wall looking like they were up to no good. My mum said, 'Why don't you plant roses and then maybe they won't sit on the wall?' So every morning I had to get up in my white dressing gown and water the roses. One time one of the guys said to me, 'I'm not being funny, but are you gay?' I said, 'Well, I am actually. Is that a problem?' He said, 'Oh no. We just wanted to know.' Now we get on really well with all the guys on the street. We've done all the murals outside, and we get people coming round on tours, taking pictures. One time the police said, 'What is this place? Is it a kindergarten?'

You expected some degree of tension when you first moved into the area, yet you were embraced. Surprised?
Well, it wasn't as easy as that. It takes time for them to respect you. One time we had a party and one of the guys threw a brick over the wall which almost hit me in the head. I went ballistic and it stopped after that. Now some of them come to the parties. I have been here for eight years and it probably took two years to settle in properly.

Would you say you've had an impact on the neighbourhood?
We probably weren't the best neighbours when I was younger. I used to go out a lot and would have big parties every Saturday night. We had a little potting shed and there was nothing in the garden but broken toilets. I wanted to build an extension, but it was really expensive. Someone told me you didn't need planning permission for wooden buildings so I just built a bigger shed and got it soundproofed. When I got the hot tub, I thought, I don't want any of the neighbours to see me getting one; they'll think I'm a wanker. Of course it didn't bloody fit, and the guy goes, 'You'll have to get a crane. You'll have to get all the neighbours to move their cars.' I said, 'You're joking!' So all the neighbours were watching and applauding when it was coming over. My worst nightmare.

Mistaken by neighbours for kindergarten decor (opposite top), murals by Alex Noble and Morris Monroe, along with various bric-a-brac signs (opposite bottom), decorate the walls outside Rothbart's home. 'We get people coming round on tours and taking pictures,' he says. Though the parties are less frequent, The Shed is no less popular or lively, with a DJ booth, lasers and smoke machines, piano, dancefloor and hot tub (left) into which Rothbart climbs 'every morning'. Showing off his Gucci boots, he takes a turn on the light-up dancefloor (below), a gift to himself for his fortieth birthday

'I'm Jewish, my neighbours are Somali, someone in this house is half-Nigerian, we've got a Polish guy and a lesbian singer'

Tell me about the concept behind The Shed.

When you finished at a club, it would be 2.00 or 3.00 in the morning and everyone would have nowhere to go. We just thought we'd have the party at the house and it became more popular. For my fortieth birthday, I got a light-up dancefloor as a present to myself and we've got a big DJ box. I'm a bit older so it's gone from a weekly party to about four or five a year. It's all harmless fun. Take for example Jacqui Potato, this drag queen who does this egg trick. He basically lays eggs out of his arse into a frying pan. So he once had to go next door to the shop in just a jock strap and buy some eggs … We did the murals too. The Council came over and said, 'It seems like gun crime has gone down a little, so we'll pay for a couple more murals if you want.'

Why all this fun, colour and effervescence here and not elsewhere in London?

I lived in Soho, which initially was fun. Now it's really boring. People are friendly here. It's got that European culture of sitting outside and drinking. It's also a bit of a cultural melting pot. I'm Jewish, my neighbours are Somali, someone in the house is half-Nigerian, we've got a Polish guy and a lesbian singer. A lot of creative people are drawn to this area from all over the world.

What do you do for a day job?

I've been working in TV for about twenty years. I've done everything from shows with Mary Portas to *The Apprentice*. I've just done a film, *Dressed as a Girl*, which celebrates East London and features The Shed. That was how I met Jonny [Woo], and out of that came The Glory, where I'm co-partner.

THIRTY THREE THIRTY THREE

THIRTY THREE

Morell Maison & Chris Vaughan, Founders

Morell Maison and Chris Vaughan behind the altar of St John-at-Hackney (opposite). **The Grade II listed eighteenth-century church, which began its life in Stepney Parish in 1275, now boasts a congregation of fourteen hundred – the largest in East London. The church welcomes a diversity of religions and ethnicities, with over 10 per cent of its members belonging to other faiths, including Buddhism, Judaism and Sikhism. After setting up music festivals in Ghana through Moringa Tree charity, Vaughan initiated experimental drone and ambient sound sessions to make use of the church's acoustics. St John Sessions have grown into a series of events mixing work by performers like sound artist Tim Hecker and musician Jon Hassell with that of younger artists such as Peckham-based Rezzett and Hackney-based Arca. With help from the visionary Father Rob, St John at Hackney now hosts films and art exhibitions amongst its music sessions and regular services. Meanwhile, Thirty Three Thirty Three utilises unusual spaces from Berlin to Beirut for performances, talks and exhibitions. 'We try and come up with stuff that no-one else has come up with,' explains Vaughan. 'That's a creative thing in itself, and we're quite arrogant about it. We don't want to be like anyone else'**

How did you both end up in London?
Chris: I'm from Suffolk and have been a part-time builder since I left school at sixteen. I moved to London after studying at Royal Holloway, where I made obscure esoteric up-my-own-arse video art and wrote about modernism.
Morell: My earliest experiences of East London were visiting my family in the late 1990s near Ridley Road. The neighbourhood was quite culturally orientated with large family gatherings and cook-outs.

How did you guys meet?
Chris: He applied for a bar job at the Peckham Pelican, which I co-owned, in 2013. I saw his CV and noticed he had worked for Boiler Room, NTS and Brownswood [Recordings] so thought he should put some music events on at the bar. It failed miserably due to sound limitations, but we became mates.

How did Thirty Three Thirty Three start?
Chris: I set up a charity with an office in the Church of St John-at-Hackney and had the idea of doing music events in the space. My friend James and I set up St John Sessions, and as its reputation grew, so did the team. We now do events beyond Hackney and have created an umbrella organisation called Thirty Three Thirty Three. We're trying to pull together the art and the music worlds.
Morell: Across unexpected areas and in different parts of the world.

Do you feel that you have succeeded?
Chris: We're getting there. We're starting to work with galleries and museums like the ICA, the V&A and Tate. We have other jobs to support this vision, and because we aren't putting money first, it has allowed us to try and come up with weird and wonderful stuff we wouldn't otherwise think about doing. I want to travel, see new things and meet interesting people … This is completely selfish!
Morell: For me, it's about a platform that allows us to express ourselves creatively rather than calling it an arts organisation.

Has having lived in and operated out of East London given you a sense of endless possibilities?
Morell: The initial inspiration was creative London, linked to diversity. I don't think something like St John Sessions could have existed outside of London and been so reputable.

'Father Rob at St John understood that there
were hipsters everywhere ... these two worlds
were colliding and he wanted St John to be
a centre for the whole community'

Chris Vaughan

Chris: Father Rob at St John understood that there were hipsters everywhere and he wanted to reach that audience. He understood that these two worlds were colliding and wanted St John to be a centre for the whole community.

What's your dream project?
Morell: Our running title is 'Museum of the Future', which would be an institution of immersion.
Chris: It's to do with the senses. It's something we took from Naoshima in Japan when visiting last year. Most art institutions focus on feeding your eyes, and there were no spaces focusing on sound. In fact, sound has almost been entirely eradicated in galleries. There should be both an audio experience as well as a visual one, including a touch-and-feel experience.

Do you feel that today's cultural world is filled with boundaries?
Morell: I'm not a big fan of labels. There's this weird middle section between escaping the industry and accepting yourself as an artist, which is a sort of boundary, I suppose, but there are different journeys for everyone.

If you had to fast forward a hundred years, what stamp would you like to have left on the world?
Chris: Nothing. I genuinely like the idea of being insignificant. I have no interest in being at the front of anything. I like being involved but not seen. I'm also selfish as fuck, that's the truth. I want to experience everything I can.
Morell: I don't necessarily care about my name, but I definitely care about the impact we have as a whole. It's hard to think about how much impact someone can have when you have people like Elon [Musk] doing some of the most amazing things known to man.

Vaughan and Maison stroll through St John-at-Hackney's walled garden, awarded Heritage Green status for the Tudor houses and gardens surrounding it (opposite). **Once unsafe and the site of the 2011 Hackney Riots, the churchyard was restored by ministers; onsite knife bins have collected more than forty-five hundred knives since then. Vaughan and Maison at Pacific Social Club** (left), **opposite the church on Lower Clapton Road. 'As long as you create something as honestly as you can, you can create in any medium or any format,' observes Maison**

TONY GRISONI

Writer & Film Director

Where are we right now?
We're on the River Lea in the Lea Navigation canal. Just over the other side is Lea Valley Marina, where there's every kind of boat you can imagine.

What is your connection to this location?
My connection is that I like water. I ended up buying this little rowing boat that I'm very fond of. When I want a break from writing, I come down here, get in the boat, row on the canal – and the world feels very far away.

Does the canal give you time to think?
Time *not* to think. You get into a rowing rhythm and you look at things that are interesting and funny. You've got hens making a nest out of twigs, bits of wire and hypodermic syringes among all the rubbish … I like the mix of water – nature – but also urban space. It feels outside the limits, a place where you're not observed. People who live here reinvent themselves.

There seems to be a recurring theme in the East, a tension between grit and glitz, a sense of living on the edge between two worlds.
It's complex, that relationship between order and disorder. I'm not a poor man, but if I had no money I'd have no protection against the disorder. Because I'm not, I can indulge in it. You have plenty of people living around here who are barely surviving. I have a lot of time for them because they're dealing with real issues.

You moved to the East from North London, right?
I'd always lived around Crouch End. Then I moved to Stoke Newington, which, twenty years ago, was still affordable. The move had very much to do with cost. We originally lived in Green Lanes where a lot of Kurdish people settled after leaving Turkey in the '70s, '80s and '90s. I liked the fact that it didn't feel like England and there was contact with people in little businesses. Around that time in Green Lanes, I witnessed a street fight involving about forty guys where someone was killed. I found out that the cause of the fight involved the local Kurdish community standing up to drug dealers.

And that led to your short film Kingsland?
Yes. I wanted to make a film informed by real stories told by real people, so we cast non-professional actors from the community. It was shot with an anamorphic lens the size of a baby, so it was a very epic format. We're now developing *Kingsland* as a TV series and I still want to cast from the community.

Tony Grisoni rows on the River Lea (opposite)**, taking a break from writing and getting away from it all. 'I came down to join the rowing club just after the Olympics, but they were full as everyone wanted to become an Olympic medal-winning rower,' he laughs. 'I ended up buying myself this very standard, rather beautifully shaped rowing boat that I'm very fond of'**

Was the film well received by the community?
Generally yes. But when you are making a film set in the Italian, Kurdish or Pakistani community, I don't think you should expect them to pat you on the back, because there's a sense of theft in some way – the idea of a photographer stealing your soul …

Did you feel you were giving back to the community in which you live?
I'd love to say yes because it would make me look good, but the truth is: No. I wanted to make a movie. If I really wanted to do something to help, I'd do something else. But I'm not a social worker, I'm a film-maker.

What is it about this neck of the woods that attracts you?
It's very varied. If you go to Spring Hill, it's mainly a Hasidic Jewish area; then you'll have an area filled with mosques. You'll go through areas which are very wealthy and areas that are shabby-chic, and in Hackney Wick everyone's making a bar from some old boxes. I feel incredibly lucky to be living in this area because you don't have to walk very far to have a very different experience. That's pretty good for living in the city. I enjoy the different tribes!

On a walk, Grisoni passes a houseboat (above) **and a shed occupied by other boating enthusiasts** (left) **in Lea Valley Marina Springfield. 'This part of London hasn't been gentrified yet, so it's a little oasis,' he notes. 'It feels outside the city limits, a place where people can reinvent themselves'**

'I like the mix of water – nature – but also
urban space. It feels outside the limits'

NATALIA TENA

Actress & Singer

Describe your relationship with the East End.
I first fell in love with it when it was a shithole. I was about twenty and lived on Murder Mile. My area was a great mix of Jewish community and Muslim community, and the main road was just mad, and had so much character. It was cheap and had loads of colour and culture. I loved it. Today, Broadway Market is fantastic, and I love Victoria Park. I love the area on a Saturday night when I am walking or cycling home and you hear great music coming from all the bars, not crap music. Passing Clouds is one of my favourite venues.

Talk to me about the music scene in the East End.
They were very welcoming when we first started out. There was nowhere we could play in West London, but the East End has always been open to new musicians. We can be different and not do mainstream stuff, and we are embraced for that.

Was acting always written in the stars?
I never thought I would be an actor. I loved it, but I thought no-one actually made a living out of it unless you are a size-2 model. I was a very angry adolescent with loads of dreads and piercings – they called me Nit at school. I use to get caught smoking. I was coming out from my favourite place to smoke when the drama teacher saw me and told me to go into the theatre barn. If you got busted smoking, you got suspended, and if you got suspended three times, you got expelled. I was already on my second suspension, so I was like, 'Noooo!' This beautiful woman arrived and said, 'Can you read this?' I read it thought, 'That was easy! I am not busted.' A month later I got a recall and it was for *About a Boy*.

You live on a canal boat and move around. Talk to me about your 'on-the-water' lifestyle.
In the old days, I hated moving house, but after about a year of living in whatever area I would get itchy feet. Now I move myself and all my stuff without having to do all that horrible moving house. I love it because you feel like you are the captain of your own world. There is a great community on the water. Whatever area you are in, you learn to love, so you spread your love of London.

Natalia Tena smokes her pipe (opposite) **in the kitchen of her houseboat, called *Fosse*. 'You are the captain of your own world,'** she says of her home, on **which she travels London's canals from King's Cross to Hackney Wick. An Agatha Christie fan since childhood, Tena takes a** reading break on her roof (above)**, noting that 'you work out which books you keep as there's no space on a boat!' Her houseboat purchase grew out of a desire to explore new places without having to move house. 'You spread your love of London,' she explains of life on the water**

Tena leans on a graffiti'd RIP dedication to 'Little Al' and beneath a CCTV heart sculpture (left) on a bridge over the River Lea in Hackney Wick. The walls of the abandoned Lord Napier Pub (opposite) are covered with graffiti works by Nemo, Himbad, Noriaki and Float. Tena pauses for refreshment at The Wick (below), a retro-style greasy spoon boasting low prices and generous portions. Though the area is changing, the café is supported by new locals and old regulars alike

'The East End has always been open to new musicians. We can be different and not do mainstream stuff and we are embraced for that'

A view from CRATE Brewery in Hackney Wick across the River Lea Navigation, which passes Tottenham, Bow, Clapton, Hackney Wick and Limehouse as it winds its way from Hertfordshire to the River Thames. Many of the thousands of canal boats that use the waterway each year moor up at Hackney Wick for a craft beer or canal-side event. Beyond that is White Post Lane, a collection of warehouses, studios and creative spaces

LEMN SISSAY

Author, Poet & Broadcaster

Your mother, Ethiopian by origin, shows up in London, and before you know it, you are transported into the foster system. Did you find solace in creativity?
That would be absolutely correct. Creativity and poetry were a way of translating my experience on a series of different levels simultaneously. It didn't matter if somebody else liked it or accepted me as part of the poetry movement. I *had* to write. It has its own momentum. An architect I once met said he can only know a building's personality after it's built. Then he'll walk inside it to know whether it's male or female. I've got to walk inside it and hear it talk back to me.

You once said that you had your soul in different places: Manchester, London's East End, Addis and New York, where your mother eventually moved.
That's right. My stories have unfolded as I've been around the world to find my family.

Isn't it true that geographical boundaries imply mental boundaries, philosophical boundaries?
Yes. Racism is what I'm talking about. It's one of the most universal traits, not because it's behaviour you're born into, but because it's learned behaviour about geographical boundaries, also about your mental, emotional and spiritual boundaries. As artists, we're boundary-less, and we experiment through our senses. It's quite a gift that we've been given, and many of us don't take it. It's there for us to explore and exploit. When we do art in the community, we are breaking with the cosiness of imposed boundaries.

What sort of mark would you like to leave on this earth of ours?
I'm tattooing myself literally into the skin of the community I live in. That can be the world of Hackney or Ethiopia. On my skin, on the walls, in the streets. It brings me closer to the community.

And closer to a collective memory?
Exactly. If you think about community as family, then I am tattooing myself into the collective memory of that family. All family is, is a group of people proving that each other exists over a lifetime. I've never had that. I have it now to a certain degree.

How does all of this fit together?
It doesn't necessarily fit. There's no master plan. We are being hypnotised into accepting our high streets and our lived environments by planning departments, by multinational companies. The poets and the artists are the true rebels in this architectural neoliberal future-speak that is happening in our world.

Lemn Sissay in front of the Bryant and May Factory in Bow (opposite), **where a largely female workforce organised the first strike action in British trade-union history, protesting poor pay and excessive and dangerous working conditions. 'You do something,'** Sissay notes, **'and it has an electricity, a strength, a vibe, and it echoes out.' He has used his poetry as a way of** 'translating experience on a series of levels'; **his poems are dotted round the streets of London and Manchester. As the first poet commissioned to write for the London Olympics, he chose to honour the women and girls of the Bryant and May strike with his poem** *Spark Catchers* (below), **which features on the electricity transformer in the Olympic Park**

'I'm literally tattooing myself into the skin
of the community I live in. On my skin,
on the walls, in the streets'

Sissay contemplates the Grade II listed factory (left) established by Francis May and William Bryant. One of London's largest match factories at the turn of the century, it has been redeveloped into Bow Quarter, a series of apartments and penthouses with fountains and a sculpture garden. 'People have become aware of the history of this building because of the poem,' explains the writer of his connection to the building. Sissay pauses at Climpson & Sons (above), one of many new establishments in Broadway Market. 'It's really important that we disrupt these consumerist environments that our communities live in,' he asserts. 'It's important that we get in the way of the narratives that unfortunately our communities have accepted'

QUEEN ELIZABETH OLYMPIC PARK

Rising out of Queen Elizabeth Olympic Park in Stratford, the *ArcelorMittal Orbit* was designed by artist Anish Kapoor and modified by artist Carsten Höller to include the world's tallest slide. Britain's largest public sculpture stands opposite Zaha Hadid's purpose-built wave-shaped aquatic centre. Much of the more than £9 billion invested in East London for the Olympics was concentrated in Stratford with the aim of creating a new metropolitan centre. Now a London transport hub, Stratford is second only to King's Cross in importance

CEDRIC CHRISTIE

Artist

Cedric Christie passes a
photograph by gallerist and
former artist Maureen Paley
in an exhibition he curated
for the Corridor Project at
White Post Café (below).
His 'Hackney Council'
embroidered jacket can
only be ordered by word
of mouth.

Christie (opposite) has
lived in East London since
1991, witnessing its shift
from an industrial area to
a residential/commercial
one. 'What enabled it to be
really creative was the lack
of accessibility to a whole
other section of society,'
he explains

Were you born and bred in the East?
No, I was born in Essex. My ex-wife and I met this guy
Wolfy who showed us an empty studio warehouse in the
East End. He said, 'Obviously, you're not going to tell me
you're living in it, but if you were, you'd sand these floors
and they'll look brilliant!' That was 1991. The only pub
open was The Bricklayers Arms. I had to pay them £300
to open on a Saturday night for my birthday party!

What were the catalysts of your creative journey?
Hackney Wick used to be an area where you could get
things made, but the public wouldn't go there. There'd be
sandblasters, rubber-cutters and print merchants, and
that was exciting to artists – industry mixed with this
can-do attitude attracted artists. Dagenham now feels like
Hackney Wick before, as you can get things engineered
and there's a clash of ideas. It's a middle-class apparition
with a working-class mentality; the two gently bump into
each other without tension. You can walk for a mile and not
find a coffee shop because no-one's going to buy a coffee
for three quid, but you can get something engineered.
There used to be a large print centre famous for
pornography, and around the corner they'd sell baguettes
but call them 'French sticks'. Artists and industry workers
mixed in cafés drinking bad coffee together.

Where do you find inspiration?
I get inspiration from the possibility of being able to
make things. I spent a lot of time with milling firms and
polishers, listening to how they solve problems. I also
trained in welding. My life is all about looking at how you
can do things differently and finding solutions. I often
compare my work to dance, which pushes your body to
that absolute limit for that one moment. I too sacrifice
everything for being great, which can be destructive as the
necessary single-mindedness can fuck with people around
you. You're chasing success in the now, and then there's
the other aspect that 'now' will pass. That's terrifying.

*You derive your art-historical knowledge from a ready-
made circle of people who've gone through the art-
education system, right?*
In the early '90s, I got a studio in Hoxton Square and was
fortunate because there was a community of artists like
Don Brown, Richard Patterson, Gary Hume and Sarah
Lucas. I didn't go to art school, so these conversations
became my art history. If I am interested in an artist, I
will know a lot about that artist, but if you ask me about
the Renaissance, I wouldn't have a clue. But I'll always ask
you to explain it to me so I can be part of the conversation.

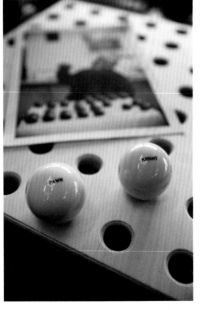

Christie amid Hackney Wick's warehouses – some done up, some not (top) – inhabited by creatives. His informal artistic education came via his early relationships with artists in buildings similar to these, among them Don Brown, Simon Liddiment, Richard Patterson, Gary Hume and Sarah Lucas. 'I hadn't gone to art school,' Christie notes. 'When I sold my first sculpture, I couldn't spell the word *sculpture*.

It was something I'd never thought about.' He holds his 2015 work *Yellow* (above) in front of Page 3 nudes layered on a wall of the JMR Section Benders office over a period of years. Christie makes and stores much of his metalwork at the steel factory in Dagenham (opposite, top), where he supplies workers with chocolate biscuits when visiting and they play on his snooker-ball chessboard, *Conflict* (2000) (left)

Christie enjoys visiting increasingly hard-to-find greasy spoons like The Griddlers in Hackney Wick (right). 'Anna's café on Rivington Street was the worst café in the world, but for £1.50 you got a bacon fry-up. It was all affordable,' he remembers. 'Stav round the corner would go through 150 baguettes – called "French sticks"! Now he barely gets through fifteen a day'

'I got a studio in Hoxton Square and was fortunate because there was a community of artists ... I didn't go to art school, so these conversations became my art history'

WARREN DENT

**Events Creative of the Bethnal Green
Working Men's Club**

*Seventeen years and you're still going strong at the
Bethnal Green Working Men's Club …*
Yeah. We opened in 2000 but were illegal for the first
five years. At first, we were just trying to keep it open
for East End members as an old members' club. It's a
traditional thing in Britain. In the Victorian era, they
made these social clubs for the poor. There wasn't any
drinking; they served as educational venues.

So now you do events and parties?
Yeah. Slowly over the years the members got used to it.
Now they may have a little moan but accept it and think
it's fun. We have the freedom to do what we want.

Can anyone attend?
Yeah. The nice thing is that we have so many different
people come so you don't just have hipsters. The gay
nights are a mixed crowd. It all feels natural and social;
everyone gets along. We've had McQueen, Florence + the
Machine and a mixture of celebs.

*What have you concentrated most of your creative
energy on?*
The transgender thing we've been working on for a long
time. Once you've seen it on TV you know the message is
coming through. Everyone's talking about it and everyone's
accepting it, so that's great. The next thing would be for
people not to ask, 'How's your boyfriend?' or 'How's your
girlfriend?' and just say, 'How's your partner?'

And the revival of Studio 54, is that a new initiative?
That's a couple of years old. We wanted to play things
that people rarely hear, maybe only in New York, and we
do it all from vinyl. One of our new initiatives is Street
Beat. We want kids who actually are from Hackney. I tell
these kids, 'Come perform and I'll pay you.' They do the
commenting, the mixing, dance-offs and competitions, and
they dance among our regular crew. It is hilarious as they
try all these moves and it just makes everyone connect.

**Warren Dent on the top
floor of the Bethnal Green
Working Men's Club
(BGWC)** (opposite)**, an East
End working men's club
open since 1887** (left)**. Dent
began curating themed
nights in 2000 but has
since expanded its social
presence as part of efforts
to stop the club's closure**

'There were so many artists in the area so we offered a space to experiment and tried to demonstrate the same ethos as the working men's club by providing cheap drinks and a good atmosphere,' he explains. His evenings range from music and performance sessions to racy club nights and cosy board-game evenings or spoken word. 'A lot of experimental stuff has come out of here,' says Dent. 'We don't care about how many people you can get in the door, we care about the ideas you have'

REPTON BOXING CLUB

Established in 1884 by Repton School to support and encourage young men in one of the country's poorest communities, Repton Boxing Club is housed in a former Victorian bathhouse and is Britain's most famous amateur boxing club.

Amateur boxer Jonathan Dfionciy (opposite) leans against the ring surrounded by photographs of former champions, press clippings and event posters (above) along with the club motto, 'No Guts No Glory'. The Kray twins and gangster Frankie Fraser were once regulars at the East End club

Heavyweight Arnold Obodai (left) **skips rope with other boxers and trainees. Located in Tower Hamlets, Repton acts as one of few local resources available to youth there. The elevated ring** (opposite) **overlooks images of famous alumni including John H. Stracey, Audley Harrison, Darren Barker and the Krays. While the busy club attracts many talented boxers** (above)**, its high Victorian ceilings and 1950s interior also attract location scouts from the film industry. For example, Guy Ritchie featured Repton in *Lock, Stock and Two Smoking Barrels***

'No Guts, No Glory'

THE APPROACH

Jake Miller & Emma Robertson, Partners & Directors

When did you start the gallery, and why in this pub?
Jake: My parents already owned three or four pubs in this area. They lived in the East End and I was looking for a space to put on some extra shows. They showed me this building, a beautiful Victorian pub with high ceilings. We only intended to do this for about a year or so.

What year are we talking about?
Jake: It was March 1997. It wasn't started as a commercial venture at all, just as an artist-run space. It wasn't until 1999 that we started representing artists. Emma started working here in 2002 and became a partner in 2012. I first thought, Maybe not above a pub is what I'm looking for, but it worked well at openings; the pub was making money and we were benefiting, so everything worked quite nicely. It was a unique place.
Emma: The pub has always had a mixture of locals and people who came to the openings. I think the gallery has always been more of a destination, less now as the area has gentrified, but people definitely do make a special journey to come here. There are also quite a few galleries in the area now so people can see a few at a time.
Jake: This place was a really big drinking pub downstairs. There were a lot of East Enders that would be watching football down there, and upstairs it would be this weird place that not many people knew about. You'd have to push your way through the crowds to get up there! Today, you go downstairs and people are ordering food in a very polite and posh way. The whole area has changed with the galleries up on Herald Street.
Emma: Sometimes you have people coming from abroad who know our gallery well from art fairs and they still are surprised when they visit. They're quite charmed as the concept is still new to them!

Emma Robertson and Jake Miller (opposite) at The Approach Tavern, the pub downstairs from their gallery on Approach Road. When he founded the experimental artist-run space, Miller only intended to use the first-floor space of his family's pub temporarily. 'Bethnal Green was the badlands back in the '80s,' he recalls, 'but by the '90s a lot of artists were living in the area.' Today the palm tree-festooned beer garden (left) hosts a different crowd from the gallery's early days. 'If anyone looked remotely trendy walking into the pub,' remembers Robertson, 'it was a really rare thing'

HENRY HUDSON

Artist

Henry Hudson prepares to delve into the tropics (opposite) **for his 2017 exhibition *Sun City Tanning*, centred on a series of works inspired by jungle-scapes, botany, transcendence and transgression – and** evocative of paintings by **Henri Rousseau. Colourful cacti** (top) **dot the artist's studio, which is filled with pallets of Plasticine** (above), **used by Hudson to compose his pictures**

We're on Roman Road. Why the name?
It was a Roman road. Boudicca came this way on a chariot to fight the Romans. Of course she was defeated and never came back.

Am I correct in saying that it was a pretty rough street until recently?
It's slowly starting to change on this side. You'll see next to me the first wine bar in the whole of Roman Road. There are a few reasons for that. The first is gentrification, which is coming over from Victoria Park and over to Bow. Secondly, until recently, power in Tower Hamlets was mainly in the hands of the predominantly Muslim Bangladeshi community, which didn't necessarily like giving out licences to bars. Eric Pickles stepped in; that's why we have this bar opening next door. Hopefully, it's the first of many.

Has the mix of cultures and religions proven to be a good thing in this area?
Having lived all over London, I love East London the most. The reason I'm here is yes, it was more economical, but actually what's brilliant is the mix of cultures. I like living here because it's so diverse. It is continually evolving and changing; it keeps me fresh. If you go to Kensington or Chelsea, it's a dead zone. People are fearful that everyone who is not wearing a tweed suit is going to rob them. I've certainly experienced that myself.

So who lives around here?
People who are into art, young people who have similar tastes, people who are at an early point in their careers, who are doing okay, who need access to Greater London. And people who have start-up businesses.

If you were to encapsulate your experience in the last couple of years in East London, how would you describe it?
As madness. Chaotic but kind of orderly somehow. I sort of enjoy the squalor. There's a method in the madness. There's a unique energy and creativity. I think the mix of cultures really helps. I really enjoy it. I went to Sweden for the first time and I was very excited because I was through passport control in fifteen minutes and into a car and it was very clean. But within an hour of being there, I'd seen no graffiti and I got bored instantly. Where's the grit and substance? Here, you don't know what's around the corner. Are there prostitutes up on that floor? Is there a bar down in that basement? Is there a start-up at that corner? You keep discovering.

'I sort of enjoy the squalor. There's a method in the madness'

Hudson uses watercolours to fill in a sketch (above) **in his Roman Road studio. The artist regularly ventures out in his neighbourhood, dotted with graffiti'd murals** (opposite) **and dominated by a market which fills the street three times a week** (right)

GINA

Owner of Gina's Closet

Gina outside her second-hand furniture, bric-a-brac and clothing shop, with artist Henry Hudson browsing in the background (right). The shop is now a relic among the small independent shops on Roman Road, having been there since 1993. Its owner Gina describes the shop as it used to be as a 'jumble sale' without so much as an official name. Now, as a result of one of Mary Portas' makeovers of commercial premises in 2013, it has a proper sign and a fresh coat of paint, and the shop looks more inviting. However, Gina is not convinced that the makeover has impacted her sales, crediting passing trade instead. Having lived in East London since she was seventeen years old, Gina has always loved the 'craziness' of the area, which she attributes to the diversity of people living there. Coming from a generation that values neighbourliness and a hospitable open-door policy, she views East London as one of the friendliest places to live in the capital

'There's a lot of characters around here, and it would be a shame for them to go. It would be a very bland place!'

JACK LEIGH

Gangster (Retired)

What is your real name?

My real name is Morris Minsky, but I'm known as Jack Leigh. I was in a business with the Kray twins, and we lived in Mile End. At one point, we had over a hundred bodyguards looking after rich Arabs in Mayfair and Hollywood stars.

What was the mood at that time?

The '60s and '70s were wonderful. The Krays were in Bethnal Green and we were in Roman Road. They never bothered us and we never bothered them. There was great respect. We all got together when the Kray twins got out of prison and made peace with the South London gang – the Richardsons. We had that famous meet-up in Broadmoor to divide London up into sections. In those days, Broadmoor was a hospital, but you could walk in with a machine gun and no-one bothered you. All you had to do was sign the book. Our eyes met, and we just burst into laughter! We were like children. It was enjoyable!

You were a gang of gangsters, but to me it sounds more like a gang of gentlemen?

There was a sense of belonging because we loved one another and relied on each other. It was all about respect and protecting our neighbourhoods. If one of the girls got hurt, word would get around and we'd sort it out because the police didn't do nothing. We never swore in front of women; we respected our families. It was a wonderful way of life, in our own way. I know we were out of the glue of governments and society, but we never put anyone in trouble. If someone went red, they'd get punished, but it had to be real bad. A lot of my crew are dead now, but there's still a few of them alive, and we have secrets that we keep to our graves.

Tell me how the gang scene changed over the years.

The drugs ruined it. You got gangs now with no respect, killing people for no reasons. We call them 'plastic gangsters'. They are not real men, not what we call 'stand-up'. A stand-up means a man's man, honest, and he won't roll over.

What mischief are you up to now?

I've started a charity shop for St John's Hospice. I'm seventy-seven now, but I'm still well respected around here.

Jack Leigh pages through *The Twins: Men of Violence*, **a book about the Kray brothers in which he features, at his granddaughter's coffee shop on Zealand Road** (opposite). **He and the Krays formed Krayleigh Enterprises, a lucrative security company that provided protection to clients including actress Barbara Windsor** (below) **and Frank Sinatra. Described in the book as a 'loveable rogue', Leigh is now long retired**

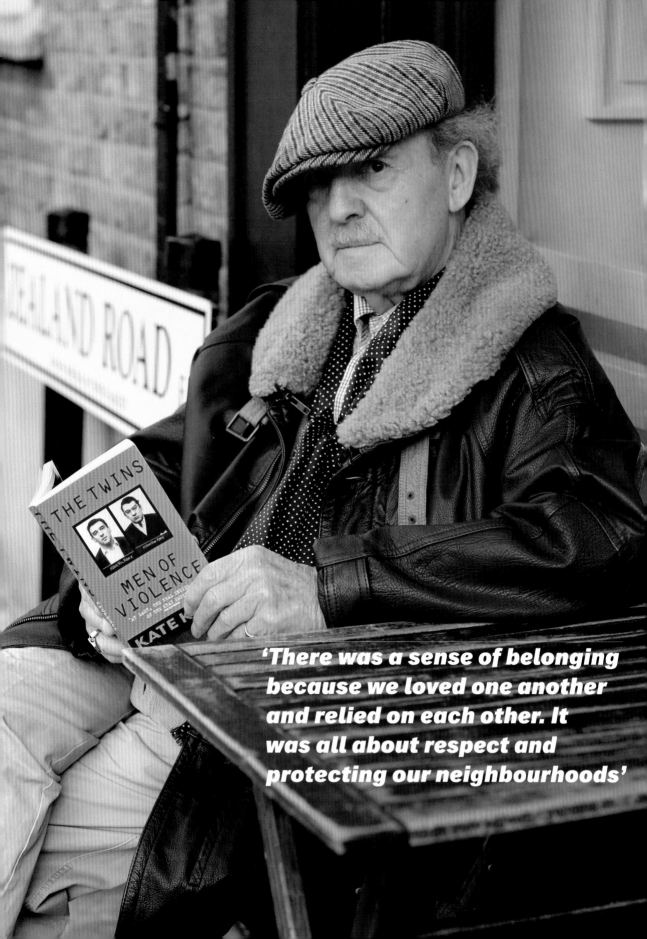

'There was a sense of belonging because we loved one another and relied on each other. It was all about respect and protecting our neighbourhoods'

G. KELLY

Pie & Mash Shop, Roman Road

'We sell pies to everybody from the real traditional East Enders to the hipster generation'

Neil Vening

Established in 1939 by George Kelly, this family-run business is now in the hands of the fourth generation. The pie-and-eel combination harks back to when street sellers peddled pea soup, pies and hot eels, with the first shops being set up in the mid-1800s. In recent years G. Kelly has seen a resurgence of popularity, and now sells pies to everybody 'from the real traditional East Enders to the hipster generation'. The pies are handmade in G. Kelly's in-house bakery using a family recipe as old as the shop itself. In the past, eels were purchased from Billingsgate, having been brought up the Thames by Dutch eel vessels. Gentrification may be changing Roman Road, but G. Kelly is one of the retail ventures that has been able to keep up with the changes. The shop is currently being refurbished, including the restoration of the original tile decor, with the interior being taken back to the 1930s

Finished in 1967, the eighty-four metres high Grade II listed Balfron Tower has been a Poplar landmark for half a century. Hungarian-born Brutalist architect Ernő Goldfinger envisioned a social housing estate which freed up the surrounding area and allowed residents to interact outdoors, with the indoor hallways designed to mimic the pavements of the East End. Falling to the capitalist axe, Balfron Tower is scheduled for redevelopment into luxury flats, an ignominious ending to Goldfinger's dreams for East Londoners

BOW ARTS TRUST

Educational Arts Charity

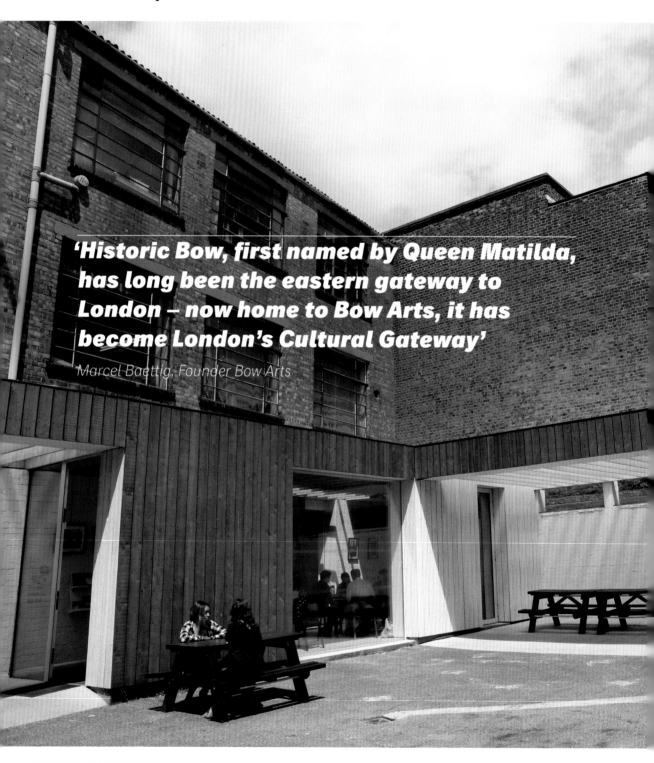

'Historic Bow, first named by Queen Matilda, has long been the eastern gateway to London – now home to Bow Arts, it has become London's Cultural Gateway'

Marcel Baettig, Founder Bow Arts

bow arts trust

BOW OPEN SHOW

BY ALEX CHINNECK

FROM 16 JUNE

NUNN E RYGALLERY

FREE ENTRY

Staff members relax in the courtyard of the Bow Arts Trust headquarters, a converted biscuit factory redesigned in 2014 by Delvendahl Martin Architects (left). The trust provides affordable studios for over 200 artists and over seventy 'Live Work/ Work Live' units for artists across Tower Hamlets and Bermondsey. Established in 1994, Bow Arts has grown to become one of the largest studio providers in the UK, with more than thirteen complexes across East London. The charity runs an exhibition programme through Nunnery Gallery, a former nineteenth-century convent within the Bow Arts complex

DEBORAH CURTIS

**Founder of The House of Fairy Tales,
a Children's Arts Charity**

Tell me about your early days in East London.
Gavin [Turk] and I have been together since art college, and we moved to lots of different parts of London in those early years. We were living in amazing squats and were homeless when our first child was born. We went to the Council, who gave us keys to this flat in Hackney Wick. It felt so far beyond the edge of the universe. Things change fast. When we moved to East London, we felt we were coming home. First, because of space, as space is such an important thing for your imagination. But also because of the historical roots of the East. I've done a lot of work with children around the history of the East. Hackney had big markets and gardens that were supplying the city, but also, as the wind was blowing east, it was used as the rubbish dump for the city. It's often been on the margins, and that's why the immigrant communities would settle here, because it was always cheaper. Now there's this interesting switch with the creative community, although I think the move for creatives is now out of London. It's an interesting challenge as the artist has become such a cliché in the development conversation. We've worked with a lot of property developers as a charity; they want the magic they get from creative people, but they don't necessarily know how to integrate that into their development projects.

Deborah Curtis atop a mountain of shredded paper (opposite) at the D. & M. Leftly and Sons recycling plant near the studio she shares with her husband, artist Gavin Turk. 'You see the extraordinary consumption that we're going through at the moment,' she says. 'The quantity is scary.' Curtis founded her charity in part because she wanted to be 'part of the solution and not part of the problem'. Encouraging children of all ages, socio-economic backgrounds and religions to take part, The House of Fairy Tales travels the nation, encouraging creative thinking by providing imaginative spaces complete with elaborate sets, costumes and fantastical objects. The charity has now outgrown its storage units (left) in East London

What was the driving force behind your charity?
The House of Fairy Tales was born out of the Port Eliot Festival in 2006. I was interested in education and in what it takes to create an inspiring environment for children. What makes creatives such wonderful people to hang out with is that they are curious about everything; there are no boundaries to their interests. They are able to find the bizarre, the surreal, and just ask questions. I felt that was something we didn't really have for children, neither in our society nor in the education system. That is what motivates me to keep doing this kind of work. I don't get paid, it takes a lot of my working hours, and it can be quite stressful because the ambition is always more than the budget. Making fantastic experiences with children is a hard thing to manage. The driving force behind my personal motivation is to be part of the solution and not part of the problem. How do we empower the next generation and make them understand that there is something worth living for and fighting for? And by 'fighting for' I don't mean conflict. It's about how we can live differently.

What is it about this part of London that's attractive to you?
I've got the most extraordinary people a stone's throw away. It's about having access to brilliant minds and networks and space. There is something of the melting pot of humanity in the people that end up in the East End, but I think that's changing at the moment. It's tougher and tougher to have a mixed community here. Still, the combination of artists, creatives, refugees, the old East Enders who have been here for generations, brings a spirit of loyalty and commitment. There's a poetry about things around here. We're working with a brilliant project at the moment: the education programme around *The Line* by Megan Piper. She's put artworks in a walk between Stratford and Greenwich. We're drawing up a creative map and a project that will be delivered in schools. The art is a small part of what we're doing, because it's about the history and geography of the area. This is also primarily a recycling area, so you see the extraordinary consumption that we're going through at the moment. From Gavin's point of view, he likes the fact that we live and work on the margins.

And the future of the charity?
The charity has moved seven or eight times over the years. We move to amazing buildings or in-between spaces given to us by property developers, and every time we inhabit the space, we end up doing lots of work with local organisations, artists and small charities, and then the space gets redeveloped and we move on. I have, on this journey, had a lot of meetings with people in government and people in decision-making echelons to know that we're on the right track and that we're in a good place to deliver a lot of constructive things.

'We've worked with a lot of property developers as a charity; they want the magic they get from creative people, but they don't necessarily know how to integrate that into their development projects'

The House of Fairy Tales logo (left), caravan (above) and travelling signage and trucks (top) await installation at a Victorian cotton mill in Manchester with an anticipated audience of sixty thousand. 'The ambition is always much more than the budget,' says Curtis, who is reviewing the viability of a permanent space in London. 'We've moved to these amazing buildings given by property developers over the years,' she explains. 'We inhabit the whole space and work with organisations and artists, and then the space gets redeveloped so we have to move on. I think we've done that six or eight times.' As for many arts organisations in the East End, the forces of redevelopment present a constant obstacle. '*Artists have become shorthand for "You drop it in the mix and it makes it all successful." It's much more fundamental than that*'

Set within the heart of the Queen Mary University campus lies Novo – New – Cemetery, the oldest Jewish burial ground in the UK with connections to the Sephardi community dating back some three centuries. Though Novo Cemetery opened in 1733 (in what was once an orchard), an earlier burial ground existed nearby. Oliver Cromwell's acceptance of Jews into England (after a 350-year absence) allowed Jewish immigrants fleeing persecution from the Iberian Peninsula into the realm. Many of the tombstones in Novo Cemetery lie flat, a feature of Sephardi burials, which symbolise equality of all humans in death

STEPHEN WEBSTER

Jewellery Designer

You were an East End pioneer, weren't you?
I did my apprenticeship in Hatton Garden at seventeen and was working with a guy who had a house off Victoria Park. He rented out rooms, and everybody who lived there was a jeweller. It was the Queen's Jubilee in 1977 and there were big street parties. Ours had a reggae band at one end and a steel band at the other end. It always felt like a really tolerant place.

How did your jewellery adventure begin?
To go to art school was my ambition, and Medway College had a strong jewellery department. I would never have thought of making jewellery. I wore it, but it wouldn't have entered my psyche. I was a punk in the late '70s. I used to have both my ears pierced, which was pretty radical. I came home once and I had dyed my hair pink (my girlfriend was a hairdresser and used me as her guinea pig). My parents were so wonderful and accepted everything. But as soon as I discovered jewellery, there was nothing else for me.

Tell me about Hatton Garden.
Hatton Garden was where you served your apprenticeship and were indentured to a master jeweller. It felt like I was always the youngest. I remember people joining the company after me, and I still had to clean the toilets. And then I'd have to get everybody's lunch! But that's where I learned all those great things which turned me into a good craftsman. It changed in the '80s, but in the '70s everything was still traditional. Everything was done with cash. I looked different, though, because it wasn't like everyone from Hatton Garden was a punk. At the market in Leather Lane I remember having fruit thrown at me. It was the most exciting thing because it felt like young people had taken charge and that seemed to make older people angry.

Stephen Webster toys with inspiration in his studio (opposite). **Named Creative Director of Garrard & Co, the world's oldest jewellery house, in 2008, Webster has kept his studio in its offices ever since. Webster on the Chinoiserie bridge** (left) **leading to the Pagoda** in Victoria Park. Designed for a Chinese exhibition in Hyde Park in 1842, the Pagoda was moved to an island in Victoria Park in 1847 and then rebuilt in 2010, after a period of decay and ruin, thanks to a Heritage Lottery Fund grant

'Hatton Garden is where I learned all the great things that turned me into a good craftsman'

When did you leave Hatton Garden?
I left in 1981 and moved to Canada. I went from a really urban life to this crazy ski-resort village in Banff. I hated it, but I stayed for a bit before moving back to England. When I got back, my mentor, who was an incredible gemmologist-adventurer, said, 'I'm moving to California; do you want to come?' So, I moved to Santa Barbara and lived there for nearly five years. Santa Barbara was not quite like Victoria Park or Hackney in 1977.

Was that your first contact with the acting set?
Yeah. My first celebrity client was Elizabeth Taylor. She picked this ring that I'd made; it had a chalcedony in it, which is a lavender stone. There was always this legend about her lavender eyes. I was making bold, colourful jewellery and didn't use other craftspeople. If I couldn't do it, I didn't do it. Taylor then commissioned a bracelet and a pair of earrings. Kirk Douglas and his family were in Santa Barbara too. They would all come down to the Biltmore Hotel and have brunch on Sundays. There was definitely a Hollywood vibe. All that old lot kind of glowed; they weren't like human beings. Goldie Hawn was also a client.

Today, you are the It Man in jewellery. What is it that inspires you?
Inspirations are literally whatever takes my fancy. Often the craziest things can become the best collections. My team are so in tune with that. If I say, 'I've been reading Blake and there's this poem where I think we can pull something out of it,' they just sit there and wait until we've done it. I recently did these chef's kitchen knives, and all the handles are sculpted beasts like a boar, a rooster, a bull, a salmon and a courgette (for vegetarians). All the blades are hand-forged in Peckham. I found these guys in a bloody railway arch, hammering out these Japanese techniques. Thomas Heatherwick had knife envy. He said, 'I love this technique! They look like they were done in Japan!' and I said, 'They were done in Peckham!' It's a pillar of our brand. We make as much as we can in England.

Are you all about craftsmanship and using your hands?
When I'm talking to students, I always make it clear that being a jewellery designer is only one element of being a jeweller. It's easy to come to art school these days and think, I'll draw it and get someone else to make it. I never even thought of drawing it; I only made it. In the end, it was through making and my exposure to working with exotic gems that I started to create a style that became mine. That's the bedrock of what we do still.

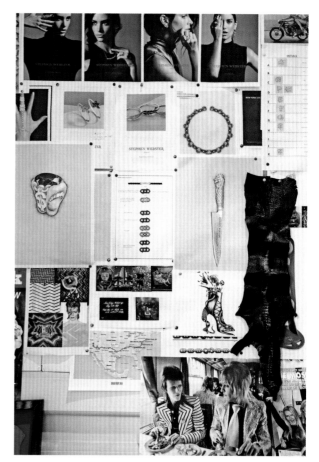

Webster contemplates avian life in Victoria Park (opposite)**, a place he visited frequently in his teenage years. 'There was a huge event in Victoria Park called Rock Against Racism where I went to see The Clash,'** he recalls. **The rock 'n' roll aesthetic of that time still influences his work, as is clear from sketches and aides-memoires pinned to the wall of his studio** (above)

MOLLY MICKLETHWAIT & RUFUS WHITE

Artists & Collectors

Describe your home and your workshop. Is it a sanctuary? A dream? A set?
Rufus: It's all of that.
Molly: It's our own oasis where we can bizarrely and realistically live all our childhood dreams.

Molly, you've lived here all your life, haven't you?
Molly: I was born just up the road and moved here before my first birthday. When we were small, the building was derelict with no glass in the windows. We used to climb inside. There were feral cats living everywhere.

Why are you both trying to hold on to this part of London?
Rufus: We look a bit bonkers holding on to it, but alongside being skint and struggling, this would just be built over by anybody else who would own it.
Molly: If we want to live anything comparable to the life we do, it would have to be out in the countryside. And then you're not in the city. We can invite it in and see it, yet at the drop of a hat we can become hermits again.

Artists Molly Micklethwait and Rufus White (opposite) in the dining room of the Factory, their home and the repository for their varied collections. 'It is a series of sets,' explains Micklethwait, whose godfather was the house-museum creator Dennis Severs. The artists' shared love of objects resulted in themed rooms such as the Music Room (left). The building's unique spaces regularly serve as backdrops for fashion shoots

'This place is our own oasis where we can bizarrely and realistically live all our childhood dreams'

Do you work separately or as a duo?
Rufus: This house has become a way of testing our work and our habits of collecting. We rent the house for photo shoots. Its eccentricity lends itself to fashion.
Molly: This means we can essentially put time into playing with our toys!

Would you call yourselves installation artists?
Rufus: My predominant job is silversmithing, Molly's a ceramist, and we collaborate on paintings.
Molly: We both work in a wide variety of disciplines and wouldn't want to limit ourselves as we enjoy the cross-pollination.

True craftsmanship and artisanship have largely been lost. Do you feel a sense of pride in the skills you've acquired?
Rufus: Yes, because in my silversmithing, I'm not using waxworks and casting them; I sculpt the silver from scratch.
Molly: I also hand-make my tiles with a rolling pin. We both enjoy being able to see something through from basic stages to the finished product. The pleasure comes from the process rather than being in a sterile atmosphere with a big power tool.

In terms of your collection, you've picked it up along the way, right?
Molly: People bring us things and gift things to the collection that might otherwise go to waste. Some things are kept for memory's sake, and others will be made into something else but still retain the story.

So you're recycling?
Rufus: In a way. All the structures are self-reclaimed. All of what you see, the way it's landscaped, the lawn and everything built, was created in the last five or six years. Both our parents had interesting friends with weird and wonderful houses, like sweet shops to go into, so this is like a sweet shop for adults!

What mark will you leave behind, do you think?
Rufus: I like the idea of leaving things for people to decipher and find.
Molly: We're leaving behind things that we have created. It's always so wonderful when somebody wants something that you've made.
Rufus: To me, it's not so much the future or what we will leave behind; it's about sharing and appreciating the now.

The Office (opposite left) **is themed in orange, grey and 'mannequins and lobsters',** explains Micklethwait, **while the outdoor areas** (below & bottom) **are nicknamed the Village and Toytown respectively. 'Anyone with a business head would have knocked this old factory building down,' notes White. In fact, most of the areas** surrounding the couple's garden (right) **have been built on or redeveloped. Micklethwait uses the Factory for creating ceramic tiles, while White works with silver** (opposite right) **in the Workshop. 'Yes, we've made it what it is,' he says of the Factory, 'but it was a wonderful place to start with'**

DENNIS SEVERS' HOUSE

Dennis Severs' House in Spitalfields evokes the life of a family of Huguenot silk weavers in the eighteenth century. Severs' intention in purchasing the building from the Spitalfields Trust and opening it to the public was that visitors might have the experience of entering a sort of three-dimensional painting of an interior from the 1700s, almost as if the inhabitants had only just departed. Severs, an American, acquired the dilapidated property in 1979 and proceeded to make it both his home and a museum

DAVID CARTER

**Interior Designer & Owner of 40 Winks,
a Boutique Hotel**

What drew you to this part of the world?
Poverty. I bought the house twenty years ago when
property was cheap. It was derelict with no roof, no floor,
no windows and no running water apart from what came
in when it rained! I had a lovely feeling about the house;
buildings communicate and whisper in my ear. I loved the
area then; it was full of colour and life. To work creatively,
I need to be surrounded by the great river of life. I love
the smells and the noise.

Is the hip factor today a good or a bad thing?
It's both good and bad. There are lots of lovely cafés, cool
shops and attractive people wandering around. On the
bad side, you see the increasing encroachment of big
luxury brands. When we opened the hotel, everyone used
to navigate with printed maps, most of which stopped
at Liverpool Street. East London didn't appear on the
map because the assumption was that no-one would
want to go there.

**David Carter poses in a
bicorne** (opposite) **in the
music room of 40 Winks,
where theatrical still lifes**
(below) **including hats,
feathers and porcelain
sculptures adorn each
room. Styling himself
as a 'Mad Hatter' in an
'oasis of eccentricity and**
beauty', Carter's four-
storey townhouse has been
a haven for the élite in
fashion and art since 2009.
'We regularly get people
describing this place as a
life-changing experience,'
he says. 'Come as a banker
and leave as a writer'

'To work creatively,
I need to be surrounded
by the great river of life.
I love the smells and
the noise'

How did you end up working in the creative industries?
I had a successful career in sales and marketing and a
flat in Islington. A photographer took some pictures of
my flat and submitted them to *World of Interiors*. They
ended up on the front cover and I got invited for lunch to
meet Min Hogg, the legendary Editor-in-Chief. She said,
'David, you're a genius! Anything you do we'll put in the
magazine!' I'd just split with this mad Italian girl, so I
decided to bugger off to France. I got my first commission
in Cherbourg. I phoned up Min; she was expecting me
to say it was a beautiful *manoir*. I replied, 'It's a dental
surgery.' Very diplomatically, she said, 'Send some
pictures in.' She loved them. It's the only dental surgery
ever to appear in a Condé Nast magazine and was titled
'Driller Filler'. The next month, my French apartment
was the magazine's front cover. The rest is history.

Would you ever leave the East End?
Possibly. My philosophy is to embrace new things. I
didn't plan to be an interior designer, I didn't plan to be a
hotelier, but now I do a lot of creative consultancy work.
I like the idea that every day is a new day. If tomorrow I
wake up and think, I don't want to do 40 Winks anymore,
I want to go and live in Marrakech, it's important to
embrace it because it's evidence that I'm a free person.
I want my life to be as full, rich and interesting as
possible. You meet someone at a party, you fall madly in
love, and then a week later you're starting a new life in
Argentina. Why not?

Carter by a daybed
(opposite) **covered in
Egyptian cotton and silk.
He describes his wood-
panelled drawing room**
(above) **as 'mad opium
den-esque' in character.
'Although being an interior
designer may appear
quite frivolous to some
people,' he says, 'I'm a
deeply serious person.' He
purchased the Queen Anne
house** (left) **twenty years**
ago in a derelict state. Built
in 1717 for wealthy naval
officers and merchants,
the home's Stepney Green
neighbours once included
Admiral Sir Dudley North
and Captain James
Cook. 'It was alive, it was
interesting, and it wasn't
all manicured and boring,'
explains Carter of the area.
'I love embarking on new
adventures; moving to East
London was an adventure'

PAUL EASTWOOD

Skullturist

Why do you call yourself a skullturist?
At an early age I was shot. I saw an X-ray of my skull in hospital. I saw the lead in my skull and since then that image has fascinated me.

Why were you shot?
Because boys are boys. I was about twelve. We were playing around and the bullet came through the eye socket, over the top, and now it's lodged in there. Generally religion tells you to be scared of skulls. In some beautiful cultures, though, it's about the skull having lived a life and retained all this knowledge – the travel and the journey. I believe in its goodness; that's why I celebrate it.

Do you talk to your skulls?
Yup. In the morning: 'I knew you'd be there. I've got something for you.' And when you go to bed, you feel at peace because you've had this thing on your lap all day and you're feeling it and watching it grow. That's the thing: you don't know when to stop. You spend a long time before you release them.

It's funny how you use the word release, *like they're people.*
Yeah. I'm fortunate that people who have purchased them are people I've had a connection with.

In a houseboat in Limehouse Basin, Paul Eastwood (opposite) **works on his skull sculptures, which are inspired by Buddhism and his travels. 'In some ancient cultures, there were head hunters because it was a form of empowerment,' Eastwood explains. 'Skulls have retained all this knowledge and the wonders of life, so we should celebrate them.' He hunts for skulls** (left) **at antique fairs or on land where deer have been culled. Human skulls are always casts from anatomical studies. Keratin, epoxy resin, reinforced plaster, acrylic, feathers and other items give Eastwood's sculptures their individual forms**

Tell me why you chose to live on the water?
I got divorced sixteen years ago, and when I was looking at flats, it made me feel claustrophobic being in those confined spaces. This is where I found a sense of freedom.

Why the East End?
I was born in Stepney. Back in the '60s, it was a shithole. I moved to Hertfordshire. I liked the greenery, but my playground, when I was old enough to do gigs and music, had to be the East End again. My heart just brought me back here. The Limehouse dock was the main hub of all the galleons, the closest port to London. There was a big wood yard here, and it was rife with the darkness of prostitution and opium.

And today?
We're being pushed out by investors that are just here for the short term. Come the weekend, there are very few lights on. That says something, doesn't it?

Doesn't it make the place feel sterile?
It's still a community. There is a hub and we're it. All those bankers can go home; we will always stay.

'It's still a community. There is a hub and we're it. All those bankers can go home; we will always stay'

Eastwood looks out over Limehouse Basin (opposite top), where he keeps his houseboat amid narrowboats, yachts and other pleasure boats (above). Created in the 1770s to connect the Thames with the River Lea, Limehouse Cut specialised in shipbuilding and lime burning for the building industry; in the 1800s it had a reputation for sordid pubs, brothels and opium dens. Eastwood on his Harley Davidson (opposite bottom), sold in order to purchase a new Ducati. 'I like the freedom of bikes,' he explains. Though his motorbiking has taken him far afield, he always returns to London. 'I don't plot a journey,' Eastwood says of his life. 'I like the road to meander'

MARIE JACOTEY

Illustrator & Artist

Marie Jacotey collects notes, drawings and images (above) **every day to make up her coloured-pencil illustrations and other artworks. Influenced by comics from a young age in her native France, Jacotey feels that her 'work fits in' in East London because 'it's quite bold and quite eccentric'. The artist** **leaves Sugarhouse Studios** (opposite) **on Stratford High Street, where she works. Built by the Turner Prize-winning collective Assemble, the retro-fitted industrial shed hosts project spaces and studios. 'It's not only artists here,' says Jacotey. 'I love the mixture of people'**

How long have you lived in London?
I came to London to study at the Royal College of Art and have been here ever since. For the last few years I've been in the Sugarhouse Studios in Bow, a series of purpose-built studios designed by the collective architects Assemble, who won the Turner Prize.

What inspires you in life?
I look at a lot of visual references. I'm a huge fan of David Hockney and Philip Guston. But I also look at other things like fashion; I love Dolce & Gabbana as well as Nina Ricci. And I look at architecture. I look at photography, and novels are a source of inspiration because I tend to write alongside my drawings.

Your writing is full of humour.
It can be quite cynical. My mother finds it depressing and other people find it really funny, so I guess I like to play on that tension between something hilarious or sad. It's how I see life, I suppose.

Tell me about working in the East End.
I love it except it's getting rather expensive. I love the mixture of people – not just artists but also curators and other creatives.

Do you ever collaborate?
All the time. For instance, I recently made a set of drawings for Assemble …

But they're tearing down the building to put in a high-rise! Is the creative community being pushed out?
It's healthy to keep moving, but maybe that's because we're still young and settling our practices. What I find stressful is the money situation. Prices are increasing year after year; it's crazy. My rent has increased at least 30 per cent in three years. But we will just make it happen somewhere further out.

You wouldn't give up being an artist?
That's not the question. The question is how to make things viable because I want to be able to do my work.

Would you ever live elsewhere, in Paris for example?
My work changed when I arrived in London but not fundamentally. I dared to explore things further. What I was doing in Paris was more contained. Whether that change happened because I was younger or whether London actually changed it, I wouldn't be able to say. But the thing I can say is that my work really fits well here, and it's not very French. The French don't have a very positive state of mind these days. So for now, I've found my place.

EDELINE LEE

Luxury Womenswear Designer

Your CV is very strong – Zac Posen in New York, McQueen and Galliano in London. When did you start your own brand?
I moved to London to attend Saint Martins. I dropped out when Zac first set up, and then went back and forth. I had a little boy so I took time out and then started my company three years ago.

Explain your attachment to the East End.
I lived near Brick Lane when I was a student. We were a row of art students living among Bangladeshis and proper old East Londoners. Now that area is like a shopping mall. We used to find things in skips for our projects. It makes me sound really old, but it's changed that quickly.

Yet in this urban chaos, your style has developed into very clean lines …
East London is not stereotypically gritty; it's something in between. I've lived in both East and West, and maybe I embody both. When I first started my brand, I was living in Notting Hill and my studio was in Ladbroke Grove. I decided to come back to the East End two years ago as I wanted to have my studio next door to where I was living. When you're an entrepreneur, you're running around all the time. The space was perfect. It's just starting to gentrify now.

Where exactly are we?
We're on the border of Limehouse and Bow. It's a three-minute walk to the river. On one side, we have three betting shops, a strip joint and a gay bathhouse, and on the other, we have a city farm, a children's theatre and the oldest church in East London. So I'm on a dividing line.

Is East London going to be your home long-term?
I think so. I am Canadian with Korean ethnicity. I've lived in New York, Paris and Italy, and identify myself as international and cosmopolitan. Most of my friends travel a lot and feel at home in more than one space; that defines our generation. I'll be a mum dropping off my kid at school, then I'll go to a gala dinner and an art event, and then I'll be in East London seeing my friend's band. Although most of the time I'll be in my pyjamas in my studio! I'm very lucky to do a job that's not a job really.

You are close with women in the art world. How did that come about?
The first women who bought my clothes were in the art world. They carry on being my constant supporters and help me survive. I also have a lot of friends in the industry.

Edeline Lee (opposite) **in her studio on Commercial Road, where she works downstairs** (above) **and lives upstairs. She returned to East London in search of a space large enough to accommodate both. Of her designs she** says, 'You're inspired by things that you hope you can express in that one second … You never can quite get it, so you want to do the next collection so you can do it better'

You'll see a lot of my clothes at Frieze, for example. Those women are aesthetically precise and aware. They need to stand out, but they don't want to look like they've walked off a catwalk. It's a particular aesthetic.

Do you think the fashion industry will be affected by Brexit?
I'm now a British citizen and I identify strongly with the UK because this is where I found myself as an adult. I also have a son who was born here. There was a survey sent out by the British Fashion Council; most designers voted overwhelmingly in favour of Remain because, by definition, what we do is international. I have shops carrying my designs in London, Paris, Dubai, Kuwait and Shanghai. I buy fabrics from France, Italy and Austria, but I make everything in the UK. So even if I'm tiny, I'm an international designer. It's implicit in what we do that fashion is a love for humanity.

Why London over any other city?
We have a set of cities we can choose from as designers. I chose London. It's beautiful no matter where you are. It has so much depth.

What sort of stamp would you like to leave on the fashion industry?
I don't think that way when I'm working. I feel lucky to have the opportunity to carry on expressing how I'm feeling about things; that's already a gift. Just to have enough to do the next collection is amazing. Of course I'd like to become more sustainable as a company, but mainly I want to keep making beautiful things.

Lee (above) **walks down Commercial Road from her studio, passing abandoned, boarded-up pharmacies, gun shops and fishmongers awaiting redevelopment, some with hand-painted signage still intact. 'You have this constant sense of movement; it's really inspired me to push forward,' Lee says of East London. 'My collections have been getting better since living here.' Derelict eateries** (opposite) **sit alongside 150-year-old pubs like The White Horse in Limehouse. Local Barbara Waller** (left) **has run the pub for the past twenty-eight years**

Originally performed at Tate Modern's Turbine Hall as part of an event series mixing African tribal dress with contemporary fashion, *Kè fila* was produced by Kezia Frederick, a London-based fashion and textile designer, in collaboration with Namsa Leuba. Here Glenn Osei-Gyimah, Amber Joy and Amie Byron Wolfe perform in Limehouse's Caird and Rayner Ltd Warehouse. An abandoned sailmaker's establishment, the space has a deserted air, with equipment stopped in its tracks. Built in 1869, it was taken over by Edward Bonar Caird and Thomas J. Rayner, who produced an apparatus for the nearby Docklands that could convert seawater into fresh water via evaporation. Never substantially altered, the building is the last remaining ship-chandler's warehouse in the East End. Multiple attempts to renovate it into offices have been inconclusive

CHARLES SAUMAREZ SMITH

Cultural Historian, Secretary & Chief Executive of the Royal Academy of Arts

Talk to me about your history in East London.

When I was a postgraduate student, we walked down Mile End Road to look for a workshop for Romilly [his wife, then a bookbinder]. There was this house in Newell Street in Limehouse. Number 13 was a big, beautiful house owned by a man who had bought it for £3,000 in 1973. He worked for Thames & Hudson and was knowledgeable about architecture and heritage. He got a job with the National Trust, so he put the house on the market. Weirdly in those days, not a lot of people wanted to live in the neighbourhood. But we desperately wanted to buy it the moment we saw it. We put in an offer for rather more than we could afford and the people he was in negotiation with immediately upped their offer. Eventually neither of us could afford what we were offering and so the whole thing collapsed. Romilly spent about six months looking for houses in East London, but we always remembered this one house. We worked out the most we could afford and I wrote to the owner, who accepted our offer. We moved there in 1982. We were incredibly happy. It was the most wonderful house. John [previous owner] had kept the character of the house beautifully. He was said to lay in bed shooting pigeons out of the window. By the early '80s there were a few pockets of great people around here,

Charles Saumarez Smith (opposite) **in his garden on Mile End Road. Saumarez Smith often walks through Stepney Green** (left), **a historic parish that was home to merchants and a Mayor of London in the thirteenth century. Today the grand houses on the east side of the green still hint at the area's historic role**

but there was a lot of run-down Council housing, and on the Isle of Dogs there was huge unemployment because of the closure of the docks. You could still see the scars from the bombing in the Second World War when a lot of the established communities in the East End had been moved out. It was exciting because it was unknown. That is why East London has always had a romance to it.

Fast forward to today in Mile End …
Stepney Green is an old village green and there is a medieval church. Stepney was the first village outside London and has what looks like a village manor house built in the 1680s. When we were in Limehouse, you could feel Canary Wharf beginning to develop. Michael von Clemm, an American banker, went down to the old banana warehouses on the Isle of Dogs and realised there was huge development potential. One of the other people who had a sense of the opportunity was Michael Heseltine. He had an ambitious view of the opportunities of development eastwards, looking at the Isle of Dogs first, then Greenwich Peninsula, which became the Dome, and then Stratford, which became the Olympics. He set up the London Docklands Development Corporation in '81 to get away from local authority control as it was the era of the free market. My view in retrospect is that London Docklands Development Corporation as a strategic authority was actually quite good. They were criticised at the time, and have been criticised since, for not doing enough about infrastructure and creating schools. It took a while, but they've done it.

You found this house through a landscape designer, I believe.
We were in Limehouse until the late '90s and moved in 2000. Our children were growing and we needed more space. I told Romilly about these two houses and she said, 'You must be mad! I am not going to live on the Mile End Road.' Luckily six months later the landscape designer asked us to their Christmas party and their house was completely amazing. The following day we started negotiations to buy what became our house. Romilly realised correctly that it was going to be the only opportunity to buy a really big place.

Your interest in architectural details is apparent in your house …
I am not going to claim any credit. When we moved it, was still quite a wreck. I remember dressing on the day of the opening of the Ondaatje Wing. You couldn't dress on the floor because it was so dirty from the ongoing renovation work, so I had to dress on the bed.

How would you define the spirit of the area today?
One has to remember that in the '80s there was a rough aspect to it. We lived next door to the churchyard and there was the occasional murder on a Saturday night. By 2000, Limehouse was quite a smart area. Canary Wharf had developed, and there was a huge amount of new housing. Stepney still had a bit more variety to it. People think the creatives move in and then the developers move in. That is not the case. It's the creatives who move in, then food moves in, and then developers move in. Food is always ahead of development. On a Saturday morning you begin to see the change in the sorts of people in the neighbourhood. People used to talk about going to Limehouse in the '80s as a bit dangerous and that you'd need a visa. One time in the mid-'80s, I walked up the canal from Limehouse to the River Lea, and I met a man with a gun who was following somebody. I never walked there again because it felt quite dangerous. Then two and half years ago, I walked the same path, and of course because of the Olympics it's all been poshed up. It made me interested in this presence of urban change.

The world looks at London for inspiration, yet there is this delicate balance between London being the centre of the universe and rising rents pushing people out.
Cities are incredibly complicated. I do think there are risks. The biggest risks are that artists move out and can't afford studio space. But artists are adventurous. My view is that they will start colonising beyond the River Lea to Dagenham, Romford. At the moment I sense artists are going to Berlin or Portugal. There are art schools here and all the galleries are here. You need something to attract people. It's a combination of affordable property, artistic infrastructure and enough people with a sense of a community.

What sort of impact do you feel you have had on the East End?
I would be a symptom rather than a cause. I would be evidence of the process of settlement.

Saumarez Smith's regular walks through East London have resulted in the publication of a collection of his blog posts about the area. He enjoys a coffee and some local fare at Foxcroft & Ginger on Mile End Road (right). **'People think the creatives move in and then the developers,'** he notes. In fact, **'food is always ahead of development'.** Saumarez Smith enters his Georgian house in Stepney Green (following spread). **Built in 1741, it was saved from demolition by The Spitalfields Trust, having been transformed into an exhaust-pipe repair garage. Saumarez Smith and his family restored the structure, knitting it back together**

'In the East End, I would be a symptom rather than a cause. I would be evidence of the process of settlement'

SUE KREITZMAN

Artist & Designer

What is a New Yorker doing in East London?
I've been in the UK for thirty-one years. My husband was offered a position as a research fellow at Cambridge University and you don't say no to that. We bought a fabulous, shabby old house in one of the Fen villages. I was there for maybe ten years while my son grew up, but it was a bad fit for me. People would cross the street if I was walking past them! I tried to calm myself down a little, but how much could I calm myself down? I'm from New York and I'm Jewish!

You've had a successful career in the food industry …
Yes. I cooked on the BBC twice a week and wrote twenty-seven cookbooks. I wrote my last book in 1998. I became a personage though not a person, and I couldn't stand the lack of real human contact.

So you moved to London?
We rented a garret just off King's Road. It was so tiny that you didn't stand in the kitchen, you wore it. There was no heating and there were a thousand stairs, but I decided I really needed to be in London. One day, I went house-hunting with my son. As soon as I got off the Tube and walked on to Roman Road, I felt like I was home. In 1967, my husband and I rented a third-hand Vespa and 'did' the East End. We became completely enamoured with it. It was shabby and rundown, very Jewish. I loved it then and I love it now. Eventually I found this place. The rest is history.

Sue Kreitzman (opposite) **dons a Lauren Shanley jacket, statement jewellery and mega-glasses in her favourite colour, red, at home. She collaborates with Shanley on many of her jackets, whose textile panels are embroidered by a South African co-operative. Kreitzman's abhorrence for muted colours translates to her home, which is filled with flamboyant, embellished assemblages** (left) **reflecting her love of Josephine Baker, Frida Kahlo, Carmen Miranda and Billie Holiday**

You've been here for almost twenty years and you've seen some changes, I bet?

It's becoming so damn gentrified that it's slowly creeping up on me. Bow is not so bad. We have several hip coffee shops, which is a hint that it's coming our way. In the old days – which actually are not so old – it was a hotbed of crazy creativity. I started to burst into art and met people like Mei-Hui Liu, one of the pioneers of the area.

Do you think of yourself as an outsider artist?

I am because I'm self-taught and work outside the mainstream. I don't like white-cube galleries but do participate in group shows in the area that I curate myself. I am not represented as I don't like the commercial aspect of art, and although I've been successful, I don't like to sell. Instead, I do a lot of swapping with my tribe. A whole art movement has sprung up around me consisting of young and old artists because we love each other's work.

You use a lot of found objects and trash in your work, don't you?

I love trash. It's stuff I find on the streets. (My husband hates it!) On my estate, people bring me stuff. Kids bring their old toys, and I have boxes of old Barbies. I like them when they're really battered because I bring them back to life and turn them into chandeliers. You wouldn't believe the things people leave at my door. I also haunt the market at Spitalfields on Thursdays and all the charity shops. It's the element of surprise that sparks your imagination.

I've had that obsessive love and need for colour since I was very young. When I moved into my first apartment in New York in 1962, I painted some of the walls red and I was so proud. My conservative mother sniffed and said, 'You'll outgrow it.' 'Hey Ma? I'm seventy-three and I still haven't outgrown it!'

Does this love for colour go hand-in-hand with a sense of optimism?

It keeps me sane. Colour, art and the friends I've made are all very protective and therapeutic. My motto is: 'Don't wear beige, it might kill you'. It's not just a slick phrase; I'm actually afraid of it. Colour to me is youth, energy and happiness.

That the female figure occupies a central role in her work is apparent throughout Kreitzman's home (opposite) and garden (right). Her 1970s ex-Council flat consists of two properties which she combined to create an extended gallery area. Her workroom in the backyard – 'the shed' (below) – is where she keeps many of her found objects, carefully catalogued and labelled. 'Creativity here is in the drinking water,' she muses of East London. 'It's in the air'

Fashion designers Florent Bidois (right) and Anne-Sophie Cochevelou (left) plan a 'Food, Fashion and Colour Extravaganza' with Kreitzman (centre) in Nobu Shoreditch's bar, located within the newly built Nobu Hotel designed by California-based Studio PCH. This is the latest addition to the world-renowned Japanese-inspired restaurant and hospitality empire founded by Nobu Matsuhisa, Robert De Niro and Meir Teper

'My motto is: "Don't wear beige, it might kill you"'

Sue Kreitzman

A TO Z: THE EAST END

A

Accessibility
Ad hoc
Affordability
Agency
Alive
Alleys
Alternative
Anti-establishment
Antiques
Arches
Artists

B

Bagels
Bangladeshi
Barbers
Bargaining
Barges
Barter
Beards
Bicycles
Bikers
Bingo
Bookshops
Boxers
Brave
Brewery
Bric-a-Brac
Bricks
Buoyant
Bustle

C

Cabbies
Cafés
Canals
Can-do
Car-boot sales
Change
Charity shops
Christians
Clubbers
Clubs
Cobblestones
Cockney cash machines
Cockneys
Coffee
Collaboration
Colour
Community
Confidence
Continuity
Cordwainers
Costume
Council estates
Co-working
Craftsmanship
Creativity
Creators
Crime
Culture
Curiosities
Curry houses
Cycling

D

Decadent
Design
Delirium
Dereliction
Developers
Dialogue
Dirty
Discover
DIY
Docks
Drag
Drugs
Dumplings
Dynamism

E

East Enders
Eccentric
Eclectic
Economical
Edgy
Effervescent
Empowered
Energetic
Entrepreneurial
Enterprising
Estuary
Evolution
Experiment
Exports
Extraordinary
Extravagant
Exuberant

F

Farmers' markets
Fashionistas
Film
Flamboyant
Flower markets
FOMO
Food banks
Foodies
Forefront
Freedom seekers
Freelancers
Fresh
Fringe

G

Galleries
Gangsters
Gatherings
Gay
Gentrification
Greasy spoons
Glitz
Graffiti
Grit
Grunge

H

Hammams
Happenings
Hedonism
Hidden
High-spirited
Hipsters
History
Homogenisation
Hot tubs
Huguenots
Hustle

I

Ideas
Identity
Imagination
Immigration
Imports
Inclusive
Independence
Individuality
Industry
Initiative
Innovation
Installation
Intense
Inspiration
Inventive
Irish

J

Jazz
Jellied eels
Jewishness
Journalism

K

Kainotophobia
Kakorrhaphiophobia
Kinetic

Lanterns
LGBTQ
Liberated
Lidos
Like-minded
Loud

Magical
Makers
Marginal
Markets
Marshes
Medieval
Melting pot
Mosques
Multiculturalism
Multi-tasking
Music halls
Muslims

Neighbourhood
Nonconformist
Noteworthy
Neurotic
New

Occult
Oddities
Olympics
Opportunity
Organic
Originality
Out-of-the-box
Outsiders
Overground

Parties
Pearlies
Performers
Perseverance
Pie-&-mash shops
Pioneers
Plague
Platforms
Pop-ups
Practical
Producers
Progression
Prostitution
Proud

Queer
Questioning

Radical
Rave
Raw
Real
Regeneration
Reinvention
Renewal
Rendezvous
Resourceful
Retro
Ripe
Roman
Rooftops
Rough

Salons
Sauna
Savvy
Sex shops
Sheesha
Silk weavers
Skateboarders
Skyscrapers
Social
Space
Spoken word
Stalls
Stimulating
Street art
Street parties
Subculture
Studios
Stylish
Swimming pools
Synagogues

Tattoo parlours
Techies
Tight
Tiles
Tolerance
Tower blocks
Tradition
Transgender
Transience
Transvestites
Tribes
Turkish

UberPool
Underground
Unit
Unoccupied buildings
Up-and-coming
Urban
Utopia

Vaudeville
Venues
Vibrant
Vietnamese
Vintage
Visionary
Vivid
Voyeurism

Warehouse
Waterways
Weavers
Working men's clubs

Xenodochial
Xenogenesis
Xenophile

YBAs
YOLO
Youthful
Yuppies

Zany
Zappy
'Zines

citizen

hotel

LETS **ADORE** And

Each

LOCAL POLICE
INFORMATION

Render Search by James Bridle
greateasternwallgallery.com

HAVE YOU SEEN

WWW.RENDER-SEARCH.COM

Render Search by James Bridle

ACKNOWLEDGEMENTS

Voices: East London is first and foremost a tribute to the people I have met on this fabulous journey of exploration into the area's heart and soul, each and every one a unique representative of the spirit of their neighbourhood. For this, my wholehearted thanks go to the personalities whose trust I was fortunate enough to gain, all of whom gave their time, shared their passions and helped make this book what it is.

It is always easy to enumerate the noteworthy people who have participated, or helped others to come to light, or been key to opening doors and giving new direction. Harder to measure is the gratitude towards my family – my husband Edward and my two wonderfully creative children Ariana and Alex. All three have had to endure the ceaseless rhythms of this journey – not to mention my constant chatter about this and that after each foray – never faltering in their enthusiasm and support.

Enormous credit is due to TransGlobe Publishing in helping create and produce *Voices*. My sincere thanks to Hossein Amirsadeghi, Publisher and Editor-in-Chief, without whose support, guidance and continuous encouragement this initiative would not have seen the light of day. For design and management of the tortuous process involved in the creation and production of such a tome, I would like to praise Roger Fawcett-Tang. Additionally, my thanks go to Consulting Editor Andrea Belloli for her exemplary and patient editorial management, and to Project Director Anne Field for her editorial and research contributions. As well as to Emily Bryson, our tireless Project Coordinator, whose research, interview transcriptions and organisational skills have been a boon to the book. Not forgetting Liz Jones, our principal proofreader.

Additional team members included Xaviera Alvarez Nordström, an early contributing Project Coordinator, as well as our transcribers Rachel Horsman, Catriona Montgomery and Ioana Stan. And thanks to Sarah Elizabeth J. Lovegrove and Jessica Cheetham, whose beautiful lips (former) and unique makeup skills (latter) helped shape the front-cover image for the book.

The Publishers wish to thank Gilbert & George for their enthusiastic contribution in mapping the scene for me in East London, a neighbourhood they have lived in and loved as much as their art. They have been dear friends to several of TransGlobe's projects over the last few years, and their poetic endorsement in their opening remarks to the book means the world to me. And thanks to Jonny Woo, a wonderful raconteur and cultural historian of his 'city', as exemplified by his poignant introductory essay.

Heartfelt gratitude also goes to three cultural regenerators of East London – Iwona Blazwick, Maureen Paley and Charles Saumarez Smith – for their counsel and historical input.

Thanks to the multitude of creatives who helped us make the book as interesting as I hope our readers will find it to be. Principal among these are Sara Blonstein, Philip Colbert, F K Ranx Germanus-Kunda and Lyall Hakaraia. Their irrepressible enthusiasm, unique connectivity and spirit of generosity will be forever remembered.

The Publishers wish to further acknowledge the contributory guidance of Hannah Barry, Kate Bryan, Charlotte Colbert, Elizabeth Davies, Andrew Dempsey, Hassan Hajjaj, Mark Hix, Tristan Hoare, Henry Hudson, Amin Jaffer, Charles Jeffrey, Nimrod Kamer, Sue Kreitzman, Catherine Lampert, Mei-Hui Liu, Gregor Muir, Peter Shelton, Emily Tsingou, Viktor Wynd and Yu Yigang.

The Publishers would also like to express appreciation to the other worthy participants and contributors to the book, including A Man to Pet, Sedem Ama, Melanie Arnold, Natasha Arselan, Clive Bennet, Ian Bodenham, Tom Burr, Amie Byron Wolfe, Django Chan-Reeves, Peter Chipchase, Liz Counsell, Lori De Mori, Jonathan Dfionciy, Jean Egbunike, Shirley Elghanian, Kally Ellis, Rosie England, Minnie Fawcett-Tang, Nina Fellman, Kezia Frederick, Jenny Fremont, Patricia Grimm, Dan Harley, Fergus Henderson, Margot Henderson, Mary Hofstetter, Tony Hornecker, Julia Huff, Kathryn Hughes, Laura Jackson, Amber Joy, Damian Kelleher, Babette Kulik, Leila McAlister, Lucy McCormack, David Milne, Morris Monroe, Alex Noble, Arnold Obodai, Glenn Osei-Gyimah, Anna Pellicci, Nevio Pellicci, Byron Pritchard, Purple PR, Steven Riseley, Roland Reynolds, Jill Robinson, Monika Schaible, Science Ltd Team, Alex Shaw, Ariana Sheehan, Joe Sweeney, Karen Tillotson, Barbara Waller and Emma Zacharia.

Maryam Eisler
London, June 2017